To all who did not survive the war in Vietnam. And those
who did. And the families who accept us as we are,
especially my own: Jill, Harry, Jennifer, Joe, and Billy,
with fondness and deep appreciation

Bob,
The book, after all,
is about home — and
all that means. One of
the most important aspects
of home, I have found, is
friendship. Peace,
Paul

AFTER
THE
STORM

A Vietnam Veteran's Reflection

PAUL DREW

Hellgate Press
Central Point, OR

After the Storm: A Vietnam Veteran's Reflection
© 1999 Paul Drew
Published by Hellgate Press

HELLGATE PRESS
P.O. Box 3727
Central Point, Oregon 97502-0032

(541) 479-9464
(541) 476-1479 fax
info@psi-research.com e-mail

Book designer: Constance C. Dickinson
Compositor: Jan O. Olsson
Cover designer: Steven Burns

Drew, Paul, 1945–
    After the storm : a Vietnam veteran's reflection / Paul Drew.
— 1st ed.
    p. cm. — (Hellgate memories)
  ISBN 1-55571-500-1 (paper)
  1. Vietnamese Conflict, 1961–1975—Personal narratives, American.
2. Drew, Paul, 1945– I. Title. II. Series: Hellgate memories series
  DS559.5 .D74 1999
  959.704'3'092—dc21
                           99-23110

Hellgate Press is an imprint of Publishing Services, Inc., an Oregon corporation doing business as PSI Research.

Printed and bound in the United States of America
First Edition 10 9 8 7 6 5 4 3 2 1

 Printed on recycled paper when available.

Contents

Part III – Combat Infantry, 1966–67

Part IV – Calm After the Storm, 1967–85

Preface

When I mustered out of the Army in July 1967, I hoped at the time simply to close that chapter of my life and walk away. And I tried to do exactly that. But I wasn't just in the Army. I was in the Army, in Vietnam, in the middle of a war. I know now that one does not simply walk away from war. Rather, for me at least, combat became a defining point in my life's story. I understand that familial, educational, and societal influences helped guide my courses of action in Vietnam, but the literal life and death decisions made in the jungle, rice paddies, and other hostile venues have given me a perspective on life, American life in particular, unique to the Vietnam veteran.

I love my country. I love democracy. But I distrust career politicians, special interest groups, religious fanatics, bigots, and bullet voters. I care deeply about parochial issues, but I try to place them within the context of the bigger picture. I enjoy escaping to the movies, but I worry about the number of people who believe what's happening on the screen is really happening. And I worry that the enduring images of Americans who served in Vietnam will have been created by actors, directors, cinematographers, and special effects artisans.

This book hopes to counterbalance that effect, to present the combat experience without Hollywoodisms: no Errol Flynn romanticism, no John Wayne heroism, no Stanley Kubrick nihilism, no Sylvester Stallone stoicism. It claims to be a statement of truth, the truth as I remember it. A memoir, mostly.

After the Storm, then, purports to be intellectually honest. And to be honest, there is much I have forgotten about my tour in Vietnam. With the exception of two base camps, at Tay Ninh and Chu Lai, for example, I don't remember the name of any village I patrolled or fought in. I could have tried to look them up, I suppose, but the place names weren't special to me then; to pretend that they are now would be to imply that historical accuracy is more important than the overall impact of the experience.

I wonder how often truth and history cohabit on our book shelves. Although chronological precision no doubt suffers in these pages, I sincerely hope that truth does not.

So what was Vietnam all about, anyway? Vietnam, the word, bears meaning far beyond the name of a country in Southeast Asia, more than just the answer to a 1950s trivia question in geography. The word has become shorthand for the Vietnam War Era, a time in the 1960s and '70s when American youth danced at home to the mantra of sex, drugs, and rock and roll.

Baby Boomers were coming of age during Vietnam and challenged the status quo in everything. Some young women expressed their desire to be free of traditional male dominance by burning their bras. Some young men protested against the system that granted those freedoms by burning their draft cards. Half a world away, Buddhist monks also used fire as a symbol of expression. They doused themselves with gasoline and set themselves ablaze to protest the war they so desperately wanted to end. Vietnam means passion.

And so, in general, *After the Storm* has little concern for actual calendar dates. On the other hand, it borrows from the writings of Vietnam's President, Ho Chi Minh, and America's Secretary of Defense, Robert S. McNamara, in order to help establish the broader geopolitical context within which my personal story was being written. I do not believe as Henry Ford did that history is bunk, but I do believe that we should leave the telling of history to historians. We hear too much speculation today by pundits and wonks about how this politician or that world leader will be viewed by history. "What will his legacy be," Sam might ask Cokie on Sunday morning with professorial aplomb.

In the modern era of instant gratification we suffer information overload from Type A media personalities who bombard us incessantly with minutiae. They have convinced each other that first is best. Thus, a half-hour before the President of the United States delivers an address, for example, every major network produces live on camera a correspondent with an advance copy of the speech who tells us what he is going to say. Or they will report that "tomorrow at noon" Representative Upandcoming will announce her candidacy for the Senate. I suppose possession of this sort of inside dope makes an outsider feel pretty important. But I would rather hear the speech without the preview and judge its contents for myself. If the congresswoman schedules a press conference to announce something, she has already announced it and I do not need to see her do it again. The newsperson's foretelling did not make me any smarter, did not enhance my life in any way.

So it is with the chronicling of history. Only after the passage of time can we comprehend the significance of most events. Remember the "invasion" of Somalia in the middle of the night? News crews from around the world had already secured the beachhead, lights and all, to record the first shots. Yet media bigwigs, not too long before that, thought little of the early reports that led us to Watergate. Can you imagine President Harry S. Truman calling a press conference the day before ordering the bombing of Hiroshima? Hardly. Somewhere in the middle of that continuum of news coverage came Vietnam.

The same Johnny-on-the-spot reporter who might have shoved a microphone in a grieving man's face in Topeka, Kansas, and said "You just lost your wife and three children in an automobile accident, Mr. Jones, tell us what is going through your mind at this moment" could now put a GI on camera and say, "You just lost half your platoon in a mortar barrage, Private Smith from Scranton, Pennsylvania, tell us what is going through your mind at this moment." Instant history: that's bunk. Reporters are not historians and news is not history. And people who are worried about their legacies should do us all a favor and live better lives in the present.

Soldiers crawling on their bellies in manure smeared rice paddies in Vietnam did not enjoy the luxury of hypothesizing about how future generations would view their actions in the war. Yet the story of Vietnam—the place, the time, the war—was written in large measure with their blood. The value of their honorable service to our country—their legacy—is, after sufficient passage of time, finally being recognized and appreciated.

Introduction

He who leaves the fight unfinished is not at peace.

Anonymous, *The Epic of Gilgamesh*

I never killed a baby. But returning on a commercial airliner from Vietnam in July 1967 to the "real world," as GIs referred euphemistically to the United States, my greatest apprehension was that protesters—hippies, probably—would scream obscene epithets at us as we deplaned in Oakland, California. I had read about that happening to others, and feared how I might react to such an outrageous greeting from people who had no idea who I was or what I had gone through. Although that scenario thankfully never materialized, for a long time, years, I worried about what would happen when sometime, somewhere, someone would jump in my face and spit, "Baby Killer!"

No one ever did. So then I worried that some non-quantified percent of the population thought all Vietnam veterans, including me, capable of indiscriminate slaughter. How dreadfully wrong, how stupid, how hurtful. It would take many years for me to sort out psychologically and intellectually what had become, unknowingly at the time, the defining period of my life. I harbored demons to be sure, those on the surface of my psyche as well as those I had suppressed for awhile. But one thing is for sure: I never killed a baby.

And for the record, I never smoked pot either.

At that precise point in my life, I wanted only to go home, to return somehow to normalcy. First, however, I needed to rediscover what it meant to be normal, to act normally. For example, my tour in the combat zone required constant accompaniment of an M-16 rifle, even in the relative safety of base camp. I felt pretty confident that in Harrison, New Jersey I wouldn't need to carry a weapon to meals or the bathroom anymore. Hell, my parents wouldn't let me have a BB gun as a kid. So "normal" no longer meant donning a steel pot and grabbing a rifle every time I moved. I discovered quickly that normal also meant that I didn't have to preface virtually every noun with an all-purpose, profane adjective, as in, "Pass the (bleep)ing salt, Mom."

Who needs another book on Vietnam, anyway? Well, frankly, I do, and I believe many others need one, too. In the quarter century or so since the withdrawal, people are losing sight of how the war affected American citizens, so-called Baby Boomers in particular. We need to recognize that Congress is no longer comprised of an abundance of white, male veterans of "The Great War." Rather it houses a cornucopia of professional politicians who, for the most part—for the male contingent, anyway—chose not to avail themselves of the opportunity to visit Southeast Asia at the government expense in their younger days.

Politics aside, the case needs to be made that Vietnam veterans were then, and are now, your neighbors, friends, and coworkers. Like my father and his generation, we interrupted normal lives to serve our country. People need to understand that we are Everyman, not Superman, and certainly not the Bogey Man. For the most part we fell victim to the draft. Make no mistake about it, however, draftees make great combat soldiers. While trudging through the jungles and rice paddies of Vietnam we fought not directly for our families and homes or to enhance professional military careers, but rather we fought principally to return home.

Yes, we cared about the repression of the South Vietnamese people. Yes, we bought into the argument about the inevitable, insidious spread of communism if Hanoi and her allies prevailed. And yes, we loved our buddies, our flag, and our country. But most of all, as young men—many just teenagers—we came to cherish the American way of life, previously taken for granted, because we now saw the worst of all human conditions: people killing other people in war. The guys in my platoon came from New Jersey, Pennsylvania, Michigan, Indiana, and Wisconsin. Barracks chatter about remembrances of home ran the gamut from Philly cheese steaks to dairy cows. Thus, our life styles differed enormously, as did our personal backgrounds and long-term aspirations. But once in Vietnam we shared what had largely been up to our conscription and overseas deployment a latent love for Americanism which bound us then, which binds us still. For diverse reasons each in his own way loved the democracy he was born into and took for granted. I suspect we all somehow wished we could help transform this Third World, agrarian nation about which we knew nearly nothing into a mini-United States of America.

Yes, that observation demonstrates incredible lack of sophistication. It was nonetheless true for me. I remember wishing during the less than leisurely voyage across the Pacific Ocean on the *General Alexander M. Patch*, a merchant marine troop ship, that while I was there, in Vietnam, the war would end, and moreover that I would play a part in bringing about the peace. I didn't necessarily want to capture Ho Chi Minh personally, although that would have been okay, but I did want there to be a decisive conclusion to my tour of duty. The dreams, you see, of this young soldier at least, were of peace, not of napalm, and B-52s, and .50 caliber machine guns, and death. Could those of my generation who protested the war so passionately and vociferously on campuses across the nation have wanted anything more? While they stayed home and marched on ivy-laced quadrangles, I left home and patrolled the jungle.

I wasn't smart enough or motivated enough during the war to keep a diary or save letters. Truth be told, I'm glad I didn't. For what I have and what I want to share in this book are the remembrances, impressions, and insights—not recycled notations—of your neighbor or classmate whose normal life was interrupted for two years and thereby changed forever. On the civilian side, having been drafted before I could vote (at the time I took the oath of service in 1965, I was nineteen going on twenty), I confess that I did not follow the geopolitical chess game in Southeast Asia. On the military side, serving in an infantry rifle platoon, I macheted my way through the jungle, often slept next to a foxhole, and burned leeches off my body with a cigarette; in other words, I didn't spend my time analyzing intelligence data in a rear echelon bunker, nor did I ever participate in a high level strategy session in a tactical operations center. I didn't drive a truck, I wasn't a cook. I was a grunt.

The point of this declaration of ordinariness is to stress that most of the more than one million Americans who went to Vietnam were just that, ordinary people. And guess what, since their return, Vietnam veterans have assimilated very nicely, thank you, into the American quilt. Although many from our ranks have experienced personal difficulties—not unlike the population at large—we are not all homeless, drug addicted, schizophrenic drifters. We raise families, teach school, fight fires, practice medicine, deliver mail, build bridges, dig ditches, design cars, assume mortgages, pay taxes. We care deeply about life and lifestyle. Because we have witnessed the desecration of another country through oppressive belligerence, we believe in the promise of America and the collective values of the American people. We cherish our freedom, and yours.

The case can certainly be made, therefore, that Vietnam veterans and their non-veteran counterparts of both genders are more alike than not. True enough. Veterans knew that all along. A problem arises, however, when some among us misuse enlistment in the armed services as a young adult as a litmus test for fitness to hold public office later in life. Many, for example, attack President Bill Clinton's successful evasion of the draft and conclude that he cannot credibly lead the world's most powerful military establishment as its commander-in-chief. On the surface, that appears reasonable. Can't the same argument be posited, however, against his sworn nemesis, former Speaker of the House Newt Gingrich, who was second in line to the presidency in our republic? The argument is just as valid, just not as politically propitious.

This veteran resents this fatuous line of reasoning because it is always made for short-term political gain while, if made or taken seriously, demonstrating a frightening lack of understanding about our democratic system. In contrast and when convenient, politicians from both major parties note Franklin D. Roosevelt's leadership qualities. I've never heard anyone citing his lack of military service as a deterrent to his ability to lead. For that matter, in what branch did Woodrow Wilson rehearse for his role as the president who led the nation into World War I? Abraham Lincoln? With the possible exception of George Washington, military service has never been a de facto prerequisite to hold high office in this country. The point no one makes is that people who served in the military during wartime, particularly those who were drafted, did so without ulterior motive. No one that I know subjected himself to the draft and the hazards of war because he knew he was going to run for public office later in life and his time in uniform would look good on his campaign literature. Would I feel better about Clinton or Gingrich or any of the rest if they had shared my time in jungle fatigues? Probably. Do I begrudge them and the legions of other national figures their positions of power because they didn't? No.

This is America, Land of the Free. Leaders at all levels of our democracy emerge, ideally, from all segments of the population. We value diversity. And although military strength enhances our stature in the world, it does not define us as a people. General Norman Swartzkopf, a "lifer" to be sure, earned our respect for his military acumen during the Gulf War, then in large measure he faded from the public spotlight. On the other hand, his superior, Chairman of the Joint Chiefs of Staff Colin Powell, another careerist, gained greater national prominence after his Army retirement because of perceived political skills and electability. (To date and, I think, to their credit, Swartzkopf and Powell have shunned the lure of office.)

Without apology for being "only" a buck sergeant squad leader at the age of 21, I recognize full well how the responsibilities of that position pale when compared to those of Swartzkopf and Powell and all the others who commanded whole armies as mature adults. So I wouldn't pretend that my service alone qualifies me over non-veterans for civilian roles such as mayor, congressperson, or president. Honorable military service in any branch, for any duration, during peace or hostility contributes to a person's overall sense of citizenship, but it is only one factor. Veterans don't hold a monopoly on patriotism. We just don't appreciate egregious exploitation of a service record, or lack of one, as so often happens in the political arena.

To answer my earlier question again, in a slightly different way: I believe the country needs, if not another book on Vietnam, a book about the war years written from the perspective of a common citizen. Regardless of the circumstances one found him or herself in during that period, we need to continue the important business of healing. We need to quit second guessing each other about motives and actions that occurred three decades ago, to focus on common goals, and to retract the wedges that divide us.

Actions during the Vietnam War era, whether they resulted in uniformed service or successful avoidance of the same, laid the groundwork for the state of the nation today. American troop departure and afterward the immediate fall of Saigon in 1975 precipitated mixed, no, confused emotions among the American people. We had never lost a war before, and we surely didn't win this one. (Joke among veterans: "I came home in '71. How about you?" "I came home in '67. We were still winning then.")

Notwithstanding its support from China and the Soviet Union, Vietnam hardly resembled the bad guys from World War II, Germany and Japan. We ruled the sky in Vietnam uncontested with our bombers and helicopters. We had bigger guns, better equipment, superior training, nicer clothes, more money. We claimed moral superiority. We were a super power. We lost.

No American delighted in the war's outcome for Americans or for the South Vietnamese. Nor did anyone feel personally responsible. The battle at home over the righteousness of the war exhausted us. Everyone wanted the war to be over, but no one, I hope, wanted us to leave in disgrace.

In some convoluted sense better left to sociologists and psychologists, many veterans felt guilty when we arrived home. Guilt is probably too strong a word, but it's the best I can do. I can't speak for other GIs, of course, but here is the basis for my feelings. I survived. No physical wounds, no Purple Heart.

When my tour ended, I wanted to go home and I did. Our newly assigned company commander, I forget his name, asked some of us who were rotating stateside to stay; he offered us promotions. (I may have survived a consecutive tour, but it would have killed my parents.) Instead, I left Vietnam in July 1967, went to work on a moving truck in August, and matriculated at Upsala College in September. I was normal again.

I buried myself in my rejuvenated life for awhile, content with the knowledge that I had done my part, served my country, fought her war. Then I took my head out of the academic sand, watched the news, read the paper, followed the war. Guys were still dying. Friends from my home town came home wounded. How could I have left when the war wasn't over? I knew how to make sense out of those blurry aerial photos that substituted for maps. I knew how to set up an ambush and call in bracketed mortar support. I knew a damned pungi pit when I saw one. I knew when to hit the ground and when to charge. My personal sense of guilt centered on the belief that by leaving Vietnam I had abandoned every soldier who came after me.

This haunted me. I was a tough guy, I thought, emotionally as well as physically. Too tough to talk with anyone about my anguish, it ate at me. Sometimes I felt like I ran out on the war, at others I felt ashamed for elevating myself, albeit privately, to would-be Savior. I didn't capture Ho Chi Minh and I couldn't stop Americans from dying. I wanted desperately to be that ordinary guy, but these thoughts denied me that comfort. I didn't want to talk about any of this to friends or relatives, although I'm sure now that they would have welcomed a chance to help, and professional counseling never entered the equation. I feared these emotions because I thought they made me weak. The courage to act that I discovered on the battlefield eluded me at home. So I drank.

Now, there's a courageous act. Rather than soberly confront my self—the me I had become, the me that was emerging. I sometimes ran away into a beer bottle. Then I felt guilty about that. Still do.

At the risk of displaying an exaggerated, arguably unwarranted, egotism, I present myself to the reader as a modern Everyman. In the medieval morality play of that name, the title character confronted Death and learned that the only other character that would accompany him into the afterlife was Good Deeds. I dare say that some of us contemplated all the deeds of our young lives—the good as well as the not so good—with a greater sense of urgency than others. The question that all of my generation needs to ask is this: During the Vietnam War, did you do the right thing?

The Vietnam era presented the opportunity for Americans to decide and thereby to choose for themselves the best path to attainment of personal fulfillment.

But the philosophical concept of the good eluded us. We couldn't determine or distinguish whether it was something we worked for or inherited. Our parents, who had lived through the Depression and World War II, sought their understanding of the good through us. They devoted their lives to protecting us from similar catastrophes. Like their parents and their parents' parents, they wanted their legacy to be a better world for their children. Education, they knew intuitively, was the key. Higher education equated to improved lifestyle.

The pursuit of a college education for Baby Boomers, therefore, was the fulfillment for many of their parents' dreams. If full-time enrollment carried the additional bonus of deferment from the draft, so be it. But for those who chose dormitory life only as an expedient escape from barracks life, I have mixed, not totally harsh, feelings. In my heart I don't believe conscientious objection to the war motivated the majority of draft avoiders. I believe, instead, they selfishly accepted our parents' legacy without assuming responsibility for leaving a benevolent one of our own.

We boast more diplomas than our parents, but that doesn't make us smarter. We make more money, but that hasn't enriched our lives. We have as a group "done better" in material terms than our parents, but we didn't really earn this status on our own. Moreover, we are the first generation in American history that cannot offer our children the wherewithal to forge a better quality of life than ours. They experience greater difficulty financing education, landing jobs in career fields for which they studied, and purchasing a home. Our divorce rate, higher than ever before in American history, has divested our children from the knowledge and comfort of traditional, nuclear family life. Too many of us speak capriciously about family values, ignoring our legacy of broken homes.

Have we members of the aptly dubbed "Me Generation" reached the pinnacle of human potential? Hardly. Would we prefer that our children pass us on the social and economic continuum of American life? Of course. For that to happen, however, we have to exert a concerted effort to replace "me" with "we" in the social consciousness. We have to embrace the presumption that personal growth flourishes when that same opportunity exists for others. A strong national economy, for example, creates jobs for many.

Sufficient time has passed since the Vietnam era for us to apply some of the lessons we should have learned. Selective Service itself, the draft, perpetuated the Me-We culture. Regardless of support for, stance against, or apathy toward the war, deferments, specifically student deferments, skewed the pool of available draftees. More than any other factor, this non-egalitarian selection process drove the spike of division into the heart of my generation. It bloated college classrooms too often with student bodies that, absent the draft, would not have wasted their time and their parents' money sitting at those desks. Those other young men who were drafted, including me, resented the system that singled us out. This was our first betrayal.

The message was simple, direct, and clear: enroll in college, whether or not you have the aptitude or inclination to study, and you are safe; join the work force after high school and your plans for your life will be postponed—and by the way, you may also, in fact, forfeit your life in a village whose name you can't pronounce. It should not be hard to see why Vietnam veterans distrust and even dislike the system that arbitrarily sent them into combat while their more fortunate contemporaries extended the exuberance of adolescence by virtue of the simple act of matriculation. As college enrollment soared and the pool of available young men ran dry, the country instituted the lottery. The ironic twist, of course, was that winners became instant losers.

The second betrayal of Vietnam veterans occurred when we came home. Not that we sought preferential treatment but, with the exception of the GI Bill which helped with tuition payments, we found ourselves playing catch up with those who stayed home, a game hopelessly stacked against us. Simply put, they enjoyed a two-year advantage in everything. They had graduated college, they were gainfully employed, and many had married. Their head start kept them ahead. We sought jobs they already held. If we found work in the same career path and competed for a promotion, their additional experience gave them the edge. Veterans become frustrated when, increasingly as the years go by, the general public forgets, ignores, or discounts the sacrifices we made during our time in service. The interruption in our lives has had chronic consequences that others cannot begin to comprehend.

And the ultimate betrayal of Vietnam veterans is the determination by many that our service was meaningless. We cannot accept that. We didn't start the war, we fought it. We participated in the republic's tradition of defending the principles of democracy abroad with non-professional soldiers. We served with honor. It is not hard to see why we detest self-indulgent, conscience cleansing memoirs such as former Secretary of Defense Robert McNamara's *In Retrospect: The Tragedy and Lessons of Vietnam* (1995) in which he discusses the futility of the war from the American point of view. By his sin of omission—not doing all in his power to bring us home—he turned his back on us then. His book today pours salt in our wounds.

I accept the honesty I perceive in McNamara's words regarding his recantation of events and conversations. But I do not accept—in fact, I resent—the hyperbolic, self-aggrandizing adjectives he accepted then and perpetuates now that he and the rest of President Kennedy's Cabinet represented "the best and the brightest" of their generation. Bullshit.

Robert McNamara served in World War II as a supply officer, not a combatant. He may have been the best damned supply person in history, maybe even the brightest; but he did not experience combat. He didn't piss in his pants in a foxhole. He never looked down the barrel of a weapon, he never drew a bead on another human being, and he never had to decide—in an instant—to pull a trigger with hostile intent. Henry Ford hired McNamara, the materiel management genius, after World War II as some sort of efficiency guru, not as a worker bee. His (McNamara's) self-proclaimed brilliance manifest itself, basically, in number crunching. And in the end, that was his contribution to the war effort in Vietnam; he reduced strategy, policy, and human life to numbers. That's the problem.

Soldiers are not widgets that roll off an assembly line. Nor are they assets to be traded or sacrificed like stocks and bonds in the open market. There is no such thing, in my view, as an "acceptable risk" when lives are at stake. No, Mr. McNamara, the best and brightest weren't playing Vietnamese checkers in Washington. You and your political cronies erred catastrophically when you transformed the war in Vietnam into a business metaphor. The real best and brightest were serving our country in camouflage fatigues, not pinstripe suits. Even though they may have had reservations about its policies, they were taking quinine to guard against malaria, not sleeping pills to get them through a restless night. They practiced quality control by rubbing monsoon rain off bullets so that their rifles wouldn't jam in a fire fight, not buffing fenders to make a sale.

It is my fervent hope that readers of this book will come to appreciate, through my experiences and perspective, the sacrifices their fellow citizens made in the past and continue to make in order to ensure freedom, democracy, and the lifestyle any American chooses to pursue. Like the righteous person who hates the sin but loves the sinner, we would do well as a nation to hate war but respect our warriors.

Part I

In the Beginning
1945–65

Chapter 1

Post-World War II
1945–50

*If only sweet Eros and the Cyprian Queen of Love ... inspire our men
with amorous longing ... we may soon be called Peacemakers ....*

Aristophanes, *Lysistrata*

While most of the world tried to rediscover life without war after Allied culminating victories over Axis powers in Europe and Asia in 1945, true world peace remained elusive. As this book concerns itself primarily with American involvement in the war in Vietnam, listen to these words of Ho Chi Minh, dated September 2, 1945, the very day Japan surrendered aboard the Battleship Missouri in Tokyo Bay:

"All men are created equal: they are endowed by their Creator with certain unalienable Rights; among these are Life, Liberty, and the pursuit of Happiness."

Sound familiar? Ho continued:

"This immortal statement was made in the Declaration of Independence of the United States of America in 1776. In a broader sense, this means: All the peoples on the earth are equal from birth, all the peoples have a right to live, to be happy and free.

"The Declaration of the French Revolution made in 1791 on the Rights of Man and the Citizen also states: 'All men are born free and with equal rights, and must always remain free and have equal rights.'

"Those are undeniable truths.

"Nevertheless, for more than eighty years, the French imperialists, abusing the standard of Liberty, Equality, and Fraternity, have violated our Fatherland and oppressed our fellow citizens. They have acted contrary to the ideals of humanity and justice . . . .

"For these reasons, we, members of the Provisional Government of the Democratic Republic of Vietnam, solemnly declare to the world that Vietnam has the right to be a free and independent country—and in fact it is so already. The entire Vietnamese people are determined to mobilize all their physical and mental strength, to sacrifice their lives and property in order to safeguard their independence and liberty." [1]

My personal story begins a month-and-a-half after this address.

I was born October 19, 1945 while Private First Class Charles Gabriel Drew, U.S. Army, was serving on the Japanese island of Okinawa, sight of one of the bloodiest battles in the Pacific Theater of Operations during World War II. My father never talked about the war in front of us kids. As far as I know, he never talked about it, period. And it wasn't until long after his death in 1974 that I thought seriously about what it must have been like for him—not necessarily the war itself, but leaving Margaret and their kids Charlie and Honey at home to go to war, and then learning from a letter that during his final stateside leave he had caused yet another twig to sprout on the Drew family tree.

Not long after the brutal fighting on Okinawa, President Harry S. Truman gave the order to level the Japanese cities of Hiroshima and Nagasaki with atomic bombs. Several near-term consequences resulted from that decision. First, it coerced the Japanese to surrender, thereby bringing about an abrupt end to the war. (Historians can argue all they like that the Japanese were on the brink of surrender anyway, rendering the bombing superfluous. Let them argue. The point remains: the Japanese surrendered on August 14, 1945, just eight days after the Enola Gay dropped its payload over Hiroshima. The fighting stopped.) The second consequence of the bombings involves this message sent to the rest of the world, particularly potential enemies of the United States, specifically the Russians: The United States has atomic capability and moreover, if provoked, it will use it. The third near-term consequence actually involves but one life. Mine.

If the war had continued in the Pacific, my father might have been killed and I would have gone through life without ever having known him. I know full well that American-made atomic bombs obliterated more than 100,000 Japanese lives.[2] I care deeply for them, just as I care deeply for the estimated 135,000 German civilians who died at Dresden and the 6,000,000 innocents Hitler sacrificed at the altar of Aryan supremacy.

In truth, however, I can only think about those lives, those deaths—those souls—in a philosophical, almost metaphysical context. The numbers associated with war time atrocities overwhelm me, the concept of genocide bewilders me, and the repetitive nature of the whole thing depresses me. Notwithstanding all the fighting and slaughter and killing during World War II, I now rejoice that the one soldier special to me came home. He didn't capture Tojo,[3] and he didn't raise Old Glory atop Mount Suribachi on Iwo Jima. He simply served his country and he came home. I'm glad we dropped the bomb.

Wars never lead to lasting peace, they just drive the vanquished underground to emerge later and fight again. Truces that stop the bleeding bring the principals to the table, so to speak, but they ignore other strong-willed ideologists who eventually demand a hearing. The Allied gerrymandering at the Treaty of Versailles in 1919 after World War I, for example, pleased the gloating victors, but the humiliation foisted upon the defeated Germans festered until their collective consciousness was plucking ripe for the chauvinism fostered by the future führer. Hitler's subsequent call for renewed nationalism in the 1920s and '30s veiled his nascent megalomania which ultimately brought about the onset of the second "great" war in Europe, just two measly decades after the declared end to the first.

But I digress. We're not yet to the Vietnam era in this narrative and, instead of progressing, I have slipped back in time. Unfortunately, I find it impossible to isolate a single action that caused a war of any size. Rather, dates marking ends of wars seem only to serve as place holders for the beginnings of new ones. Having said that, we can observe that wars around the globe punctuate the twentieth century; indeed they shape, perhaps even define, our entire history. World War I belied its billing as "The War to End All Wars," and World War II also failed to eradicate the phenomenon, despite the decisive Allied victories in Europe and the Pacific. Nonetheless, World War II did end and my father returned. He, like so many GIs who had experienced the horror of war in foreign lands, pursued relentlessly, maybe obsessively, his and my mother's version of the American dream which as a minimum included a peaceful and hopefully prosperous family life. Working for the prosperity of their children became the goal of their generation.

Although the war officially ended, the biggest "boom" was about to be heard: the Baby Boom. Renewed focus on family life looked so good to so many war-weary couples that it spawned hyperactivity in maternity wards across the country. The Baby Boomers, swathed and coddled in their parents' post-war optimism, began arriving in numbers roughly equal to the number of returning husbands and soon-to-be-husbands. "Without war, life will be good again," Charlie and Margaret and all the reacquainted Charlies and Margarets in America must have thought. And it was. For a time. Too short a time for many.

Chapter 2

Korea
1950–53

. . . they walk ahead into the darkness, and they do not come back.

Ursula K. Le Guin, *The Ones Who Walk Away from Omelas*

By the time I made my First Communion at age seven, American citizen-soldiers had dug in again on hostile Asian ground. This time, 1950–53, the U.S.-backed United Nations instituted a police action against the Red China-backed North Korean communists who had disturbed the peace and threatened worse. (If we avoid the word "war," you see, we circumvent the constitutional requirement of having Congress sanction the action. Men can be sent, funds can be spent. All of that is semantic bullshit, of course. It was war. Ask anyone who was there. Ask a Gold Star Mother.)

More than a quarter million American men fought in Korea, many of them recalled to active duty after having served in World War II. False sense of security. Double jeopardy. Deferred pursuit of the dream. Nearly 160,000 total American casualties, 23,300 dead.

Meanwhile in Vietnam, on July 25, 1950, President Ho Chi Minh answered questions put to him by the press. Of course press conferences as we know them in the free world were then and are now unknown in communist states. Nonetheless, even via this orchestrated forum, we can gain insight into Ho's attitudes and agenda. Remember, this is 1950.

"Question: What is, Mr. President, the present situation of the U.S. imperialists' interventionist policy in Indochina?

"Answer: The U.S. imperialists have of late openly interfered in Indochina's affairs. It is with their money and weapons and their instructions that the French colonialists have been waging war in Vietnam, Cambodia, and Laos ....

"Question: What measure shall we take against them?

"Answer: To gain independence, we, the Indochinese people, must defeat the French colonialists, our number-one enemy. At the same time, we will struggle against the U.S. interventionists. The deeper their influence, the more powerful are our solidarity and our struggle. We will expose their maneuvers before all our people, especially those living in areas under their control. We will expose all those who serve as lackeys for the U.S. imperialists to coerce, deceive, and divide our people.

"The close solidarity between the peoples of Vietnam, Cambodia, and Laos constitutes a force capable of defeating the French colonialists and the U.S. interventionists. The U.S. imperialists failed in China, they will fail in Indochina.

"We are still laboring under great difficulties but victory will certainly be ours" (*Ho*, 183–84).

Blood letting continued in both Vietnam and Korea during the early 1950s. Did America really care?

Since war was never officially declared in Korea, neither was peace. Fighting nevertheless ceased in July 1953. But the battle line remains in 1998 and armed soldiers from both camps still stare stoically at each other across No Man's Land, Panmunjon, where the truce was signed. Maintaining a military presence in South Korea to deter communist expansion for over forty years has cost American taxpayers billions of dollars. For the less economically resourceful North Koreans, the perpetuation of the face saving effort flies in the face of sensibility. While the country should be waging war against the famine that is sucking away its life at the close of the twentieth century,[4] instead it refuses to admit that its political and economic systems, theorized by Marks and Engels in the nineteenth century, have failed and, worse, its leaders refuse humanitarian assistance that would save the lives of its own people. So in Orwellian double speak, because war was never declared, an undeclared war cannot end, and therefore there never was a war—just a police action. Twenty-three thousand, three hundred Americans died in uniform between 1950 and 1953 serving the cause of democracy in Korea. The war that never was, coming on a half-century later, continues to drain U.S. dollars and waste Korean lives.

From a Child's Eyes

In July 1953 when the fighting stopped, I was seven, going on eight. I don't remember playing war as a kid, although I probably did, and if I did the toys were most likely World War II vintage not Korean War replicas. My mother's cousin Pat received a medal for heroism in Korea, but I didn't even know he was there (not that a second grader would have known where "there" was). She didn't tell me about brave Pat Hesketh until I was a soldier myself twelve or thirteen years later. I was a child in 1953, afraid of the dark not of dying in a trench. My hero was the Lone Ranger, not Audie Murphy. The country, it seems to me now, conducted much of its international policy after World War II and through the 1950s with similar childlike naïveté. Because we feared the darkness of ominous, godless communism, we sent thousands of men to their deaths to stop its spread. At home we hardly acknowledged the departure of our men. When they returned, to a great degree, we ignored the personal sacrifices they made in our name. Today, many rightly refer to the euphemistically dubbed police action in Korea as "The Forgotten War." As long as we could conscript, arm, and deploy young men somewhere, anywhere, overseas to stymie heathen Marxist/Leninist zeal, the rest of us could feel safe. We did not need to be reminded constantly that our boys were over there, wherever there was.

As a child during the Korean War (now one of four, brother Paschal having arrived in December 1947), it didn't matter to me at the time that to support our family my father commuted by bus and train six days a week to a Greenwich Village basement workshop where he repaired and renewed office furniture. I not only accepted his sacrifice, I expected it. Likewise, it didn't matter much to most Americans that their countrymen overseas lost fingers and toes to frostbite, that so many thousands watched helplessly as their bodies wasted away in prisoner-of-war camps in North Korea, that so many died. If it wasn't their brother or father or lover or husband who didn't fight in a war that never was, and their lifestyle didn't change because distant battles didn't really affect them personally, most Americans pursuing "the dream" must have thought, what's the big deal?

Human beings die premature, unnatural deaths in combat. That's the big deal.

The circa 5th century B.C. Chinese philosopher and military strategist Sun Tzu wrote in *The Art of Warfare* that the object of war is not to kill men, the object of war is to kill evil.[5] We—the Allies, the good guys—joined forces in World War II to smite the totalitarian evils of Nazism, fascism, and the Yellow Peril. In pursuit of this honorable goal, we successfully transmogrified our enemies from people to heretics to heresies. Germans and Japanese became Gerries and Japs and then caricatures of Nazism and expansionism. Having subdued these evils in 1945, in 1950 we—the Allies, the good guys, this time under the aegis of the United Nations—confronted the evil of Chinese-inspired communism as it threatened to penetrate the 38th parallel in Korea and spew lava-like into the South.

The prepubescent boy I was in the early '50s would prefer to fight a bully's little brother than the bully himself. American politicians were similarly loath to challenge head-to-head the vast, amorphous source of our fear and hate: China or Russia, Chinese or Russians, communists, atheists; we would rather take a stand at a fixed location against what we calculated to be at the time a lesser opponent, a beatable foe. Thirty-seven months and hundreds of thousands of casualties on both sides later, our stand, and also by the way theirs, ended in stalemate. Both sides rationalized their efforts. United States-led United Nations forces avoided direct confrontation with the bully, China, which all believed could have precipitated a third world war, perhaps a nuclear war. From the other point of view, outgunned David-san from North Korea stood up to the American Goliath. No war, no peace; no advance, no retreat; no victory, no defeat. Sacrifice life, save face.

Meanwhile, President Ho Chi Minh reported to the National Assembly of the Democratic Republic of Vietnam which was held December 1–4, 1953. He said, in part:

> "... The Soviet Union, a bulwark of world peace and democracy, is strongly marching forward from socialism to Communism. The happiness dreamt of by mankind for so many centuries is gradually being realized in one-sixth of the world.

> "To safeguard world peace, the Soviet Union also possesses A-bombs and H-bombs, but it has time and again proposed their banning . . . .

> "China has gained a great victory in fighting the United States and helping Korea . . ." (*Ho*, 234–35).

Remember, this is 1953.

Chapter 3

Air Raid Drills
1954-57

Yet from those flames / No light, but rather darkness visible.

John Milton, *Paradise Lost*

As the conflict in Korea simmered and the Cold War escalated, I was still just a kid. Not much to say, really, about the bulk of my grammar school days with relation to Vietnam and the war to come. Kids need to do kid things, and that's what I did during those, for an American child, idyllic times. Fractions, decimals, "i" before "e" except after "c" and in words sounding like "a" as in "neighbor" and "weigh," Little League, box ball, recess, lunch at Grandma's, the Palmer method, 25 cartoons at the Warner Theater on Saturday afternoon. Kids shouldn't have to think about, much less worry about, geopolitics and war.

With all due acknowledgment to the appropriately innocent environment within which my contemporaries and I grew up, we did not live totally in a cocoon. The fifties, after all and despite relative national affluence in the post-World War II era (Korea had already been pretty much ignored, if not yet forgotten), saw ever increasing tension between the world's two surviving super powers, the United States and Russia. The Cold War between us consumed the entire decade. Some good came of the competition, particularly advances in science culminating in the latter part of the decade when, to our dismay, the Russians launched Sputnik in October 1957. We countered with Explorer 1 in January 1958. The Space Race was on and the scientific community has never looked back.

It wasn't good for us that we finished second in a two-man race for space. Worse, in my opinion, was when, earlier in the decade (1954), Senator Joseph McCarthy's (R., Wisconsin) anti-communism ran amok. He turned decent Americans against decent Americans in a witch-hunt pursued relentlessly under the august auspices of the United States Senate. Although McCarthy's self-indulgent passion inflicted more harm on the American people than good, fear of communism and even just the threat of another world war allowed him and his misguided inquisition to gain more prominence than they deserved.

Less than a decade prior to the McCarthy hearings, the righteous United States had proved its willingness to use (in today's parlance) weapons of mass destruction. If for no other reason, it was reasonable to believe that the amoral Russians would do the same—with less provocation. Japan had blind-sided us at Pearl Harbor in their bid for Asian supremacy, what was to prevent Russia from doing the same to some densely populated region on one of our coasts?

The Sisters of Charity at Holy Cross Grammar School readied us against attack. They ran us through two drills: one if we heard the air raid siren, the other if enemy planes were in sight. Whenever the siren screamed, we filed quickly and orderly out of the classroom, proceeded along the wall and down the corridor to the stairwell, and ended at a predetermined section—along a wall which we faced—in the basement. If caught upstairs during an attack, we were to lay on the floor face down under our desks and cover our heads; this would at least protect our eyes from flying glass. I wonder what the adults must have thought at the time, because these exercises carried no more weight for grade schoolers than fire drills. Every morning after we recited the Pledge of Allegiance we prayed collectively for world peace. During air raid simulations, we secretly prayed for extended drills, because anything—presumably even the possible end of the world—was better than sitting in class.

Graffiti of the '60s captured the absurdity of all this. Scrawled on many a bathroom wall were words to this effect: In case of nuclear attack, bend over, grab your ankles, place your head between your knees, and kiss your ass goodbye.

Sorry, Sister.

Chapter 4

Cuba
1958–59

It was everything to me to think well of one man,
And he ... has turned out wholly vile.

Euripides, *Medea*

The no-decision in Korea heightened American paranoia about communism. If nothing else, we had at least succeeded in sticking our finger in the Korean dike; but the red tide continued to seep through the Kremlin wall, settling in puddles of socialism around the world. Although the acronym NIMBY (not in my back yard) came into the language long after the 1950s,[6] the concept applies to American attitudes toward the unabashed entrenchment of communism in Cuba with Fidel Castro's revolutionary rise to power in 1959. Communism anywhere in the world somehow threatened capitalism. While it had spread to China in a big way, and France, Poland, and elsewhere in less noxious doses, its appearance in Cuba—our back yard—caused grave concern.

For whatever reason, America misjudged the rebel Castro who rallied the down-trodden Cuban people against the evil dictator Fulgencio Batista y Zaldivar. Castro loved baseball, for goodness sake, how bad could he be? Like so many charismatic, English speaking despots we have supported or whose human rights records we have ignored in recent history (the Shah of Iran comes quickly to mind), Castro's revolutionary spirit captured our hearts, if not our brains. After all, American revolutionists of the eighteenth century wrote the book on over-throwing tyranny. Who could say that Fidel Castro wasn't the George Washington of the Caribbean?

During the spring of my seventh grade at Holy Cross Grammar School, 1958, I received the Sacrament of Confirmation. Thus I declared before God, my family, and my congregation that I was mature enough to stand up and declare my faith by myself, just as my godparents, Aunt Peg and Uncle Jim, had done for me at my Baptism twelve years earlier. No longer child-like in my faith, I willingly and with great pride accepted full responsibility for my actions and chose freely to live by the precepts of the Roman Catholic tradition. Not quite a teenager yet, in my own mind and with Uncle Joe's strong right hand on my shoulder as my chosen sponsor, I became a man. To prepare for this rite of initiation all three seventh grades rehearsed the hymn "Onward Christian Soldiers" for weeks in the gym; through sheer repetition it evolved from song to mantra. From Confirmation Day forward not only had I abandoned childhood to embrace manhood, I had become a soldier, a defender of the faith. I was now prepared to venture boldly onward into life, to stand bravely alongside Saints Peter and Paul, Stephen, Gregory, and Joan; Mary Magdeline, Veronica, and the Blessed Virgin; Pope Pious XII. Lofty company to be sure, but through the phenomenon of my voluntary membership in the Mystical Body I belonged with history's litany of saints. Fidel Castro shook that faith several months later.

Appearing in a filmed interview on the Ed Sullivan Show as a grizzly bearded *muy macho* soldier of the people, Castro appealed to the American public for sympathy for his noble cause. He showed graphic photographs of Batista-ordered torture. They made me cringe. I remember one in particular that showed a flogged, naked man hanging by his wrists from a tree. This, Castro explained unemotionally, exemplified the brutality of Batista's rule. The picture evoked a previously unknown emotion that nauseated me. I didn't know much about Cuba or the Cubans, just what we learned in geography: location, an island nation in the West Indies; capital, Havana; crops, tobacco and sugar cane; language, Spanish; religion, predominantly Roman Catholic. Roman Catholic! How could one defender of the faith torture another? Had the torturers forgotten the promises they made at Confirmation? I felt somehow naked myself and vulnerable because of the shock, confusion, and fear the photos produced in me.

I doubted the sincerity of my own faith. Why hadn't I ever felt this deeply when I knelt before the figure of Christ on the cross in church? He suffered and died for my sins, I was taught. I personally contributed to His pain. Why did this nameless, faceless Cuban deserve to suffer and die; and why did his wretched image move me more than the hundreds of crucifixes and paintings of Christ in anguish I had seen before? How could one Christian order another's pain? At least Christ's tormentors were pagans, I thought. I shuddered alone in my bunk bed at this first concrete image of real evil in the world. I buried my face in my pillow and cried. I prayed daily that God would help Fidel Castro liberate the Cuban people from the satanic Batista, and I prayed that no one else would be tortured. More than that, I prayed that I would never see another picture like the one of the man on the tree.

I think back now to the symbolism of that dangling, mangled wretch. Was this Castro's Christ, or was he intended to represent the entire suffering nation? Did Batista's blatant, inhumane atrocities truly offend the suppliant jungle fighter's religious convictions, or was the display merely intended to assault ours? Castro the Crusader, or Castro the Manipulator? If the former, when did his crusade end and tyranny begin? Does power really corrupt, or was he power-driven all along?

Even at thirteen I understood now that evil, no longer for me simply a cat-echetical concept, really did exist in the world; but I felt helpless against it. How awful to enter manhood as a eunuch. I couldn't do that. A soldier, a defender of the faith couldn't do that. I wouldn't have shouted with the crowd, "Give us Barabbas." If Simon of Cyrene hadn't picked up the cross, I would have. Had I been there, I would have thrown rocks at the Roman soldiers gambling on Gol-gotha for His clothes. I'd go down to Cuba right now to join Fidel and Che and their glory-bound freedom fighters. Viva Castro! That's how a boy could reclaim his manhood.

Not for me. Not this time. Not yet.

God answered my prayers: Castro proclaimed himself Undisputed Heavy-weight Champion of Cuba. (Maybe this young Christian soldier armed with the power of prayer did help after all.) But soon after his hasty ascension to absolute power he forced many of his countrymen to their knees praying for *his* over-throw. America showed little-to-no interest in involving itself overtly in either the defense or overthrow of the Batista government. One dictator for another, so what? We considered Cuba not much more than a warm weather escape for Ernest Hemingway wannabe deep sea fishermen and glitter-happy gamblers who frolicked in her U.S. Mafia-controlled casinos. Leave Cuba's internal affairs to the Cubans.

It would have been fine to leave well enough alone. So what if Castro imposed oppressive socialism on his own people? Float the sport fishing boats, keep the roulette wheels spinning, we don't care. But no, he had to solicit ideo-logical and, ultimately, financial and military support for his perpetual revolution from those damned heathen Russians. That was too big a step over the line of acceptability for President John F. Kennedy who said, in effect, "NIMBY!" Kennedy's Irish-American stubbornness met Castro's Latino *machismo* head on. He suffered a setback at the Bay of Pigs in April 1961,[7] then scored big with his stance on what has come to be known as the Cuban Missile Crisis (October 1962). Kennedy exposed Castro as a Kremlin puppet and forced Soviet Premier Nikita Khrushchev to withdraw his nuclear weapons from Cuban ports. The biggest of the good guys reestablished its role as superpower protector of the free world.

Meanwhile, Ho Chi Minh saw things differently. On November 2, 1966 he reflected on the early years of the Cuban Revolution in a speech at a banquet honoring a visiting Cuban delegation, attended by Fidel Castro's brother Raúl and led by President Osvaldo Dorticós.

"... The Vietnamese people feel greatly inspired to have such a staunch, valiant comrade in arms as the brotherly Cuban people, who are standing shoulder to shoulder with them on the front line against the U.S. imperialists.

"Eight years ago, under the leadership of their national hero, Fidel Castro Ruz, and through a long and arduous armed struggle, the Cuban people overthrew the dictatorial regime of Batista—a lackey of the U.S. imperialists—brought the Cuban revolution to victory, and built the first socialist country in Latin America ....

"Under the leadership of the Communist Party of Cuba and the Cuban Revolutionary Government, the Cuban people have struggled fearlessly and recorded many successes: routing the U.S. aggressors at Giron Beach, defeating the economic embargo, and crushing all other schemes of provocation and sabotage by the U.S. imperialists ....

"Dear comrades and friends, we believe that your present visit to Vietnam will help further strengthen the unshakable militant solidarity between the peoples of our two countries and will bring us many new successes, just as is said in a slogan of the brotherly Cuban people: Vietnam and Cuba united, we shall win!" (*Ho*, 346–49).

Chapter 5

Ho Chi Minh, J. F. K., and the Domino Theory

1960–63

Things are brewing, it appears.

Albert Camus, *The Guest*

About the same time Castro seized control of Cuba, America was sending military advisors to a little known former French colony in Southeast Asia. The French had milked Vietnam (as well as Laos and Cambodia, known collectively as Indochina) of its natural resources for years but were summarily ousted in 1954 at the Battle of Dien Bien Phu. This rebellion at one push pin on the map mattered little to most of the world, it seemed. With the passage of time, however, Vietnam's most vocal and militant critic of the French, Ho Chi Minh, had returned from exile in 1945 to lead the resistance and brought back with him an unabashed, almost uncontrollable love for the brand of communism he had refined abroad.

America did not believe at first that the internal politics of this agrarian nation compromised its strategic interests in the region. Alas, however, Ho preached relentlessly about the virtues of communism, placing his successful revolution against Western imperialism within the context of the Bolshevik Revolution in 1917, and went about spreading the gospel according to Vladimir Ilyich Lenin.

United States Secretary of Defense at the time, Robert S. McNamara, recalled in his book, *In Retrospect*, how the "best and the brightest" assessed Ho: "We ... totally underestimated the nationalist aspect of Ho Chi Minh's movement. We saw him first as a Communist and only second as a Vietnamese nationalist" (*IR*, 33).[8] As preface to this remark, McNamara writes in Chapter Two, The Early Years: January 19, 1961–August 23, 1963, "I knew some things about the recent history of Indochina, particularly Vietnam. I knew that Ho Chi Minh, a Communist, had begun efforts to free the country from French rule after World War I. I knew that Japan had occupied the country during World War II; I knew that Ho Chi Minh had declared Vietnam's independence after Japan's surrender but that the United States had acquiesced to France's return to Indochina for fear that a Franco-American split would make it harder to contain Soviet expansion in Europe. In fact, during the decade just past, we had subsidized French military action against Ho's forces, which were in turn supported by the Chinese. And I knew that the United States viewed Indochina as a necessary part of our containment policy—an important bulwark in the Cold War" (*IR*, 31).

Excuse me, Mr. Secretary, but as a high school student at the time I knew all of this—some of it too well. Despite John F. Kennedy, as *deus ex machina*, plucking you from Ford Motor Company's boardroom and dropping you into the Pentagon's war room, it sure seems now that you really didn't know much. Oh, you knew how to count beyond your fingers and toes without a calculator. You could strategize and prioritize with the best of "the best." But you didn't know diddly-squat about what motivates people, even more nationalistic communists, to hunker down for the long haul.

So here's what I think. In my view, Ho would have posed little threat to the free world had he remained at home in Vietnam more or less as a provincial icon. He had returned from exile, inspired his people, and ousted a foreign invader. His heroism and formidable accomplishments were real. Communism for him, however, had become more than a system that he felt would serve his people well. His professed adherence to the principles of the Soviet prototype formed in him a world view. He envisioned more than one nation, Vietnam, united under the umbrella of Russian communism. His grand view included one world swearing allegiance to the Kremlin. Make no mistake about it, Ho was not an idle dreamer. This was an intelligent, charismatic, courageous man of conviction whose perspective on twentieth century world history was shaped on the one hand by the oppression of colonialism in his native land and on the other by the inspiration he found in similar struggles abroad. He viewed himself as a national leader, yes, but not a maverick.

On September 5, 1960, Ho addressed the Third National Congress of the Vietnam Worker's Party at which he extended a "warm welcome" to his comrades from the Soviet Union, China, Albania, Bulgaria, Poland, Germany, Hungary, Mongolia, Rumania, Korea, Czechoslovakia, France (yes, France), India, Indonesia, Japan, Canada, "and other fraternal Communist parties" (*Ho*, 313). After the welcome, he began: "Prompted by lofty sentiments of international brotherhood, our comrades have come to take part in our Congress and to bring to us the friendship of the fraternal Parties. Though frontiers and mountains stand between us, Proletarians of the whole world come together as one family" (*Ho*, 313–14).

Lest there be any doubt, I state unequivocally that I believed then and I believe now that Ho Chi Minh's world view was wrong, and as a megalocommunist he needed to be challenged. Having said that, however, there is no denying that, even in exile, he pursued his view for his country and the world with great passion. In contrast, McNamara cites his credential thus: "... I ... had served as a young officer in World War II. President Kennedy knew I would bring to the military techniques of management from the business world, much as my Harvard colleagues and I had done as statistical control officers in the war" (*IR*, 3). Excuse me again, Mr. Statistical Control Officer, but your techniques of management from the business world sucked. The moment you or any of your Harvard colleagues viewed any man on the ground as less than a human being ("assets"; I hate that term), you betrayed us. Ho, the embodiment of our enemy, used words like "brotherhood," "friendship," and "family," while America's best and brightest were proselytizing management techniques.

I recognize that many U.S. leaders, although self-indulged, weren't stupid. Kennedy and his advisors rightly recognized Ho as a dangerous zealot for the cause of global revolution. His victory over a Western industrialized country at the hands of rice farmers fifteen years earlier, if set as an example and followed by other countries in the Pacific rim, would upset the tenuous balance of super power in favor of the bad guys. The Domino Theory, it was called: if Vietnam fell to communism, so would every other country in the region in rapid succession, one after the other.[9]

I was much more interested in sports than dominoes from 1959 to 1963, my high school years which coincidentally spanned most of Kennedy's ill-fated presidency. A full-fledged teenager, I reassessed my previous claim to manhood at my age twelve Confirmation. Real manhood now meant earning a varsity letter.

Good things happened at St. Benedict's Prep in Newark, New Jersey: often good teaching, sometimes learning. Nevertheless, hormones and physical development dominate all other facets of life in any high schooler. Castro and Cuba and that woeful figure of a tortured man drifted into my subconscious. Between pimple popping and pushups, we translated Caesar, Cicero, and Virgil (not very well in my case). And forgot "Onward Christian Soldiers"; although we dutifully went through the motions freshman year of learning the alma mater, Father John's music room really rocked when we boomed out the school's fight song, "Boolah, Boolah":

> Boolah, boolah. Boolah, boolah.
>
> It's the war cry of the Grey Bees.
>
> We will down them, we will crown them
>
> Till they holler, boolah-boo. Rah! Rah!

Parents often tell their children that their teen years in high school are the best of their lives. In many ways, not all ways, they are right. While trying to muster enough courage to ask a girl to dance is hell, for example, the dance itself can be heavenly. While our parents worked to pay the rent and feed the family, our part-time jobs paid off as pure spending money. We had a war cry at the "bee hive," but no literal enemy. We read J. Edgar Hoover's *Masters of Deceit* and discussed the evils of communism and dialectical materialism (I had successfully sublimated the specific evils of Cuban tyranny by then). I remember writing an essay senior year that supported United States presence in some place called Vietnam. Three years later I was there. I had passed rapidly from what might have been the best years of my life to what could have been the last.

Here's how smart I was toward the end of those best years of my life. I was two-time indoor hurdle champion of the New Jersey Catholic Track Conference. Every year conference champions and runners-up populated an all-star team that traveled to the United States Military Academy at West Point in the spring to compete against the Plebes. I won that meet both times: 1962 and 1963. The Academy expressed an interest in me my senior year and asked that I apply.

The undeclared war in Vietnam in 1963 had absolutely nothing to do with my decision not to apply. I just could not picture myself marching around all day in a uniform, polishing shoes all night, and barking in my sleep, "Yes, sir. No, sir. Right away, sir," not to mention the fact that I had never even shot a BB gun. If I had availed myself of that opportunity (no guarantee of admission expressed or implied) and graduated from the United States Military Academy, I would have entered active duty in 1967 as a twenty-one-year-old second lieutenant. Instead, for reasons explained later, the draft sucked me up in 1965 and spit me out as a nineteen-year-old private.

During that same time frame, "the summer and fall of 1963," McNamara writes, "columnists Walter Lippmann and James Reston suggested consideration be given to neutralization (in Vietnam)." He goes on to say that "journalist David Halberstam, who reported for *The New York Times* from South Vietnam during the early 1960s" expressed "hawkish views" which "reflected the opinion of the majority of journalists at the time" (*IR*, 71–72). I had no idea at seventeen who was responsible for formulating U.S. military policy in Vietnam, or anywhere else for that matter. In middle age I read the then Secretary of Defense's book and found out he was quoting newspapermen. Not quite betrayal, Mr. Harvard graduate, but I'd trust you more, even in retrospect, if your research reached beyond mass media. Hell, you could have at least been reading the speeches of Ho Chi Minh. They were available.

Chapter 6

College, Factory Work, and Running

1964–65

There are two kinds of rat, / The hungry and the fat;
The fat ones happily stay at home, / But the hungry ones set out to roam.

Heinrich Heine, *The Migratory Rats*

I attended Manhattan College in 1963–64 on an athletic scholarship, a 100% grant-in-aid. I ran in all the track meets held at the old Madison Square Garden on Eighth Avenue in 1964, and even tied the dual meet record in the 60-yard hurdles against the United States Military Academy at West Point.

As a seventeen-year-old high school senior I didn't have a clue about what I wanted to study or what I wanted to be when I grew up. At the coach's suggestion, I enrolled in Manhattan College's School of Business. Less than one week in accounting class convinced me that business was not for me. The track coach, Jim McHugh, sent me to his predecessor, then Dean of Men, who convinced me to tough out the semester, drop accounting, and add another English course in the spring. At the end of the year, he advised, I could change my major to liberal arts, if that's what I wanted to do. Sounded reasonable. I followed his plan.

One glitch. The Dean of the School of Arts and Sciences didn't like students transferring into his program from another school within the college. It made him feel like he was second choice, he said. I refused to beg this guy to let me into his department, so I quit. I still wasn't sure what I wanted to be when I grew up, but a business major at Manhattan College definitely wasn't it. Neither was being a beggar.

I went right back to lugging furniture for H. Mace Co. Around September I landed a no-collar laborer's job as a United Auto Worker in a roller bearing plant of Hyatt, a division of General Motors. That year, 1964–65, by day I shoveled mud out of grinding machines and fought a losing battle against oil drippings at the base of huge sheet metal presses; by night I attended Jersey City State College. Crazy things rattled around in my mind that year. The focus of my life up to that point, to be honest, had been competitive sports. In high school, in addition to being conference champion, I won the indoor and outdoor state championships. While at Manhattan I ran against 1960 Olympic Champion Hayes Jones in the semi-finals of the Millrose Games and in the spring won the Junior Metropolitan Championship on Randall's Island, New York. And then I left, abruptly. Coach McHugh's last words to me over the phone went something like, "You can come back today, and we'll get you into the School of Arts and Sciences. If you don't, you'll never run again."

God, I loved to run. More than that, I loved to compete. In a pay telephone booth outside a diner with a moving van parked close by I surrendered it all. Eighteen-going-on-nineteen sure is a stubborn age—perhaps just another example of my intelligence. My gut told me that running wasn't reason enough to stay in school. Ironically, the shift from full-time student-athlete to full-time factory worker, part-time student, ex-athlete who would never run again fostered in me a greater appreciation for learning. The college's full name was Jersey City State Teachers College. Teachers, I figured, also coached. In my spare time that year I tried to keep in shape.

While I was finally discovering a sense of direction in my life, President Lyndon B. Johnson found himself caught in a dilemma about which way to go in Vietnam. The Kennedy assassination—which I heard about just before going into my Friday afternoon economics class, another brutal experience for me that first semester at Manhattan—bequeathed to Johnson policies he might not necessarily have supported wholeheartedly as vice president. Carryover advisors from Kennedy's administration, including and especially Secretary of Defense Robert S. McNamara, convinced him to escalate. Johnson increased the cadre of advisors from 16,000 to 23,000 in 1964. That number in 1965 was 70,000 and growing. By 1966, there were 300,000 of us searching in the jungle for nobody knew how many of "them." During the geometric escalation, McNamara admits, "we never fully debated what U.S. force would ultimately be required, what our chances of success would be, or what the political, military, financial, and human costs would be if we provided it. Indeed, these basic questions went unexamined" (*IR*, 107). So much for bringing "to the military techniques of management from the business world" (*IR*, 3).

McNamara shifts accountability for the escalation to the Joint Chiefs of Staff who "recommended that we broaden the war to include U.S. air attacks on North Vietnam and shift from training the South Vietnamese to carrying out the war in both South and North Vietnam with U.S. combat forces. This recommendation for what, in effect, constituted a revolutionary change in U.S. policy rested on an exposition of two and a half pages, with little analysis or supporting rationale" (*IR*, 109). Was this another lapse in management technique, or hadn't the Harvard faculty taught analysis in its business school? Still rationalizing the non-professionalism and almost anti-intellectualism apparently rampant in Johnson's Cabinet and war rooms, McNamara whines: "If we had more Asia experts around us, perhaps we would not have been so simpleminded about China and Vietnam. We had that expertise available during the Cuban Missile Crisis; in general, we had it available when we dealt with Soviet affairs; but we lacked it when dealing with Southeast Asia" (*IR*, 117). So, when people were dying, why didn't the whole bunch of you get off your lazy asses and seek out the true best and brightest? Were you academic overachievers afraid of being upstaged?

Well, let's see, a short recap here. While McNamara and his cronies stroked their over-educated egos in their corner offices of power, I struggled to find direction in my life. I didn't pursue West Point because I didn't want to be a soldier. I didn't stay at Manhattan because I didn't want to be just a runner. I didn't return to Manhattan because I flat out didn't know what I wanted to be. At last, after a year in the factory with two semesters of night school added to my year at Manhattan under my belt, thoughts of becoming a teacher and coach began to crystallize. Pop. Crackle. Snap.

During the summer of 1965, I received my greetings from Uncle Sam, and on October 6, having successfully turned my head and coughed—the toughest prerequisite for induction at the time—I became US51592530. The private first class clerk who typed up my identification card in Fort Dix, New Jersey eradicated my middle initial "J" (which stood for Joseph, the name I took at Confirmation in honor of my sponsor, Uncle Joe) and I became Private Paul Drew, NMI (no middle initial). Onward Christian Soldier, indeed.

Part II

Preparing for War, Going to War

1965–66

Chapter 7

Upping the Ante
1964–65

While I was shoveling mud out of grinding machines and mopping oil around gigantic drill press machines on the day shift and going to night school, the Johnson Administration was looking for an expeditious way to get out of Vietnam. McNamara claims in Chapter Six, "The 1964 Election and Its Aftermath: August 8, 1964– January 27, 1965," that "... Johnson had made the goal in Vietnam crystal clear. 'Win the war!' ... He never deviated from that objective. But we could never show him how to win at an acceptable cost or an acceptable risk" (*IR*, 147). Now there's a phrase that really pisses me off: "acceptable cost." Whose death, Mr. McNamara, was acceptable; and to whom? Can you tell us that person's name? Was he a colonel or a private? Did he leave parents, a wife, a lover? Silly questions.

"The Joint Chiefs agreed," McNamara continued, "we should prepare plans for U.S. air strikes against North Vietnamese targets and the Ho Chi Minh

Trail with the objective of destroying Hanoi's will to fight and its ability to continue to supply the Vietcong." (I'm sure this all looked good on papers marked "Confidential" and "Top Secret." But I'm more sure that no one in the decision making loop advised listening to Ho, the voice of the enemy. He claimed defiantly that his forces would fight to the last man for their cause.)

"That (plan), in conjunction with our later ground effort, eventually became the military strategy we followed in subsequent years. Neither then nor later did the chiefs fully assess the probability of achieving these objectives, how long it might take, or what it would cost in lives lost, resources expended, and risks incurred" (*IR*, 152). To his belated credit, McNamara admits that, "all the services (and I, as well) greatly underestimated Hanoi's determination, endurance, and ability to reinforce and expand Vietcong strength in the South" (*IR*, 153). But estimating, and other non-specific skills, is what you bean counting types are supposed to be good at. Nearly 60,000 American deaths later, he concludes: "It is clear that disengagement was the course we should have chosen. We did not" (*IR*, 164). Because your "we" underestimated, you placed the infinitely more important "we" at unwarranted risk and forced us and the American people to pay unacceptable costs. We were betrayed.

McNamara notes that, "Between January 28 and July 28, 1965, President Johnson confronted the issues spelled out in our memorandum and made the fateful choices that locked the United States onto a path of massive military intervention in Vietnam ..." (*IR*, 169). "All of us," he continues, "should have anticipated the need for U.S. ground forces when the first combat aircraft went to South Vietnam—but we did not" (*IR*, 175). Was any of this doubt, ignorance, or speculation conveyed to the American people? McNamara's memoir is filled with Monday morning quarterbacking. Unfortunately, the grunts on the ground weren't playing games.

Chapter 8

Ho Chi Minh's Charge of Imperialism
1965–66

Battles, the horrors of fratricidal war, the fever of doubtful news, the fitful events;
These come to me days and nights and go from me again
But they are not the Me myself.

Walt Whitman, *Song of Myself*

While the American military brain trust guesstimated and underestimated, Ho preached. Following are excerpts of "U.S. Imperialists, Get Out of South Vietnam!" an address President Ho Chi Minh gave to the National Assembly, printed in the *Vietnam Courier* (Hanoi), April 15, 1965, nearly six months before I was drafted.

"... Over the past ten years, the U.S. imperialists and their henchmen have carried out an extremely ruthless war and have caused much grief to our compatriots in South Vietnam .... They hope that by resorting to the force of weapons they can compel our 30 million compatriots to become their slaves. But they are grossly mistaken. They will certainly meet with ignominious defeat ....

"U.S. President Johnson has ... threatened to resort to violence to subdue our people. This is a mere foolish illusion. Our people will definitely never be subjugated.

"... The McNamara Plan has also gone bankrupt. The 'escalation' plan which the U.S. imperialists are now endeavoring to carry out in North Vietnam will certainly fail, too. The U.S. imperialists may send in dozens of thousands more U.S. officers and men and make all-out efforts to drag more troops of their satellite countries into this criminal war, but our army and people are resolved to fight and defeat them ..." (*Ho*, 325–26).

I didn't know any U.S. imperialists personally in 1965, but I was definitely one of the dozens of thousands of men about to fulfill Ho's prophecy. The disconcerting aspect of this is that Ho obviously studied American policy and strategy, such as it was, but our guys didn't take the time or exert any effort studying his.

"The American people," Ho said, "have been duped by the propaganda of their government, which has extorted from them billions of dollars to throw into the crater of war. Thousands of American youths—their sons and brothers—have met a tragic death or have been pitifully wounded on the Vietnamese battlefields thousands of miles from the United States. At present, many mass organizations and individuals in the United States are demanding that their government at once stop this unjust war and withdraw U.S. troops from South Vietnam. Our people are resolved to drive away the U.S. imperialists, our sworn enemy. But we always express our friendship with the progressive American people" (*Ho*, 327).

I couldn't pick an imperialist, or a communist, out of a line-up then—or now, for that matter. Who the hell was he talking about?

"... The U.S. imperialists must respect the Geneva Agreements and withdraw from South Vietnam" Ho argued. "That is the only way to solve the problem of war in Vietnam, to carry out the 1954 Geneva Agreements, to defend the peace in the Indochinese and Southeast Asian countries. There is no other solution. That is the answer of our people and Government to the U.S. imperialists ....

"On the battlefield against the U.S. aggressors, our people's task is very heavy but also very glorious.

"At present, to oppose the United States and save the country is the most sacred task of every Vietnamese patriot ....

"Let all of us single-mindedly unite as one man and be determined to defeat the U.S. aggressors!

"For the future of our Fatherland, for the happiness of our people, let all compatriots and fighters throughout the country valiantly march forward!" (*Ho*, 327–28).

I don't recall any American leader preaching loudly and proudly to our country at the time about glory and sacred tasks in Vietnam.

Two months after Ho's address on June 16, 1965, McNamara was asked at a press conference, "Do you foresee a build-up beyond the 70,000 to 75,000 man level?" He replied, "The Secretary of State and I and the President have repeatedly said that we will do whatever is necessary to achieve our objective in South Vietnam .... I can only give that answer to your question." The press corps pressed him: "What is the overall American strategy?" He answered, "Our objective, our strategy is to convince the North Vietnamese that their Communist-inspired, directed, and supported guerrilla action to overthrow the established government in the South cannot be achieved, and then to negotiate for the future peace and security of that country" (*IR*, 190).

He didn't convince anyone, least of all Lyndon Johnson who said on June 21, 1965,

"'... I don't believe they're ever goin' to quit. And I don't see ... that we have any ... plan for victory militarily or diplomatically .... I do not think we can get out of there with our treaty like it is and with what all we said, and I think it would just lose us face in the world, and I just shudder to think what all of 'em would say?'

"The president felt tortured," McNamara reports (*IR*, 191). Nonetheless, we stayed ... and I got drafted.

Chapter 9

Caught in the Draft
1965–66

You may relish him more in the soldier than in the scholar.

Shakespeare, *Othello*

I spent the first two weeks of my military career at Fort Dix, New Jersey. Most recruits spend a couple of days at an induction center, get their clothes, take a few tests, and ship out to a basic training facility. The whole gang of us who took the oath of service on October 6, 1965 in Newark, however, got to stay in the Garden State an extra fortnight. We found out later that the Army had selected us to populate the newly reactivated 196th Light Infantry Brigade at Fort Devens, Massachusetts, which wasn't quite ready to receive us. Typical of the Army, however, they didn't tell us anything about why we were lingering at Fort Dix. Not even privates yet—they called us "yard birds"—our waking hours were occupied with either KP or some other menial policing activities such as picking up cigarette butts and miscellaneous human droppings on the sacred grounds of Fort Dix. Now and then we would pass a huge bronze statue of a soldier with a rifle, an infantryman—the "ultimate weapon," the plaque read— and wonder what that was all about.

One morning, a never-before-seen Latino lieutenant stood before the mob (we gathered loosely in lines, but didn't resemble anything military, like a platoon or a company) and told us to get back into the barracks and "chit, chower, chave, and chine your choes, and be back out here in less than an hour." We stuffed all worldly belongings into two duffel bags. They then herded us into horse trailers that took us, scrunched duffel bag to duffel bag, to buses that transported us to Fort Devens five or six hours away.

One might reasonably question the horse trailer part. Why couldn't the buses drive up to the barracks, just as the larger, more cumbersome semis had? Not to worry. In a mere two weeks we yard birds had already accepted the doctrine of the three ways of doing things: the right way, the wrong way, and the Army way. I think now the horse trailer incident probably served one of two quite logical purposes, from the Army's perspective: 1) they were training truck drivers at Fort Dix; or 2) they were performing a psychology experiment to determine if treating ultimate-weapons-to-be like animals would make us act that way.

Mind you, this was October, fall, heading toward the New England winter, and we were jaunting off to our jungle warfare training site, the Army way. An ironic twist to this turn of events is that Fort Devens was already the home of an Army Intelligence school. I started to think, OK, maybe I'm not so smart, being just a yard bird and all, but the words army and intelligence don't belong in the same sentence either.

Another irony befell us when, early on, we discovered that light infantry doesn't mean light in any usual sense of that word. Light in Armyspeak means the soldier carries everything he needs to patrol, to fight, to eat, to sleep, to clean, even to wipe his ass. Light means heavy. And clumsy. We became horse and wagon and rider all in one olive drab package. Maybe those truckers at Fort Dix had it right, after all.

Shortly after we completed basic training, McNamara reports that on "December 30, the president expressed irritation with the Joint Chiefs' repeated pleas for permission to bomb the North. 'Every time I get military recommendations,' he pointedly reminded Max, 'it calls for large-scale bombing. I have never felt that this war will be won from the air .... What is much more needed and would be more effective is ... appropriate military strength on the ground .... I am ready to look with great favor on that kind of increased American effort.' This suggestion for large-scale deployment of U.S. ground troops came from out of the blue" (*IR*, 165).

Bullshit! Our brigade was already formed and well into formal training. McNamara then credits Maxwell Taylor as responding "with one of the most comprehensive and thoughtful analyses we received from Saigon during the seven years I wrestled with Vietnam .... He (Max) then turned to the question of ground combat, cautioning the president that, by a standard military rule of thumb, defeating the Vietcong would require a massive deployment of troops ..." (*IR*, 165). Vietnam, here we come.

Jungle Training U.S. Army Style

We ventured outside Fort Devens occasionally for various large scale training exercises, to Camp Edwards, near Cape Cod adjacent to Otis Air Force Base, and to Camp Drum, somewhere near the Canadian border in upstate New York. Trust me on this one. In January, February, and March—even April, it snowed on Easter—these North American woods, or woods like them whose wintry beauty inspired Thoreau and Frost in more serene times, in no way resembled the tropical garden spots that awaited us in Southeast Asia. Once again, lest we should forget, the Army way.

No kidding. We "raided" our first mock Viet Cong village at Camp Drum in the freaking snow. Once when my squad went out on a night patrol exercise in one of those crazy places—in the snow—we had to ford a waist-deep stream. By the time we made it back to base camp in the morning our fatigues were literally frozen stiff. We built a fire and stripped in order to thaw our clothes over the open flames. Maybe that's what "light" infantry meant.

One night Eddie Zahn and I shared a foxhole in the frozen jungle of the Great American Northeast. I may not have assimilated much military intelligence by then, but I was smart enough to align myself with Eddie, an honest to goodness woodsman from Michigan's Upper Peninsula. We had the best damn two-man foxhole in the world, no thanks to me. It had a main pit, of course, deep enough and wide enough for both of us to stand comfortably with a lit can of Sterno between us, and a waist-high ledge to hold our ammunition. Eddie also dug a perpendicular trench about five-and-a-half feet long and a-foot-and-a-half deep so that the guy who was not on watch could lie down, sleep if he could, and not be seen, or shot from the ground if this were the real thing. Eddie's master stroke was a generous layer of pine needles strewn liberally on the floor of the pit so our feet wouldn't get damp, and more along the length of the bed. (Eddie proved just as resourceful in the real jungle.)

So here's what happened. We traded watch every hour or two, I forget exactly, one of us alert in the hole, the other lying in the trench. Eddie had the last watch before dawn and my six-foot body stretched face down along the length of the bed—well, most of it, all except for my booted feet which extended past the sleeping compartment and dangled toes first into the hole. Eddie woke me at first light but my feet didn't respond. I kept popping up and falling over like a Shmoo, one of those plastic blow-up punching bag dolls with a sand base, for about fifteen minutes. Between the frigid air and stifled circulation my feet went numb with pins and needles. Jungle survival training was proving tougher than I thought it would be.

Snow Balls?

With all that cold weather jungle training behind us, the Army started to play head games again, similar to the two-week limbo-like Fort Dix experience. Long range patrols, ambushes, raids, rappelling, map reading, all that good stuff. Seemed pretty clear we were headed for Vietnam. Bod-a-boom! All of a sudden they shoved in two weeks of riot training . . . in the snow. The second platoon, my platoon, stomped down the middle of the street, shoulder to shoulder with fixed bayonets, and got pelted with snow balls by the aggressors from the first platoon.

It turns out Santo Domingo was in a state of civil unrest at the time, so the easy to believe rumor circulated that we were headed there. Since the Army doesn't make a whole lot of sense a whole lot of the time to the enlisted ranks, we didn't bother trying to rationalize why the Government had spent an enormous amount of money camouflaging huge chunks of Massachusetts and upstate New York all winter so that we could pretend we were traipsing through the jungle only to send us to the Caribbean after two weeks of ducking snow balls.

So here's what didn't happen. We didn't deploy to the Dominican Republic. Probably because there was no snow in the forecast.

Diversions

We spent the late spring of 1966 at Fort Devens, still not knowing for sure where we were going and not doing much soldiering. Someone selected me to stand next to an M-14 rifle displayed on a table at a static weapons exposition in the Worcester, Massachusetts Town Hall. That gave me a few days to do nothing but starch a uniform about as stiff as the one I wore the night we went swimming in sub-freezing weather, polish my boots until my fingers got sore, and become an expert on the weapon that the Army would take away from me and replace a couple of weeks later with the M-16.

They found all kinds of good things for us to do after completion of our formal training. My platoon marched in the Memorial Day parade in Plymouth.

Someone said we would be able to stay a few hours after the parade and mingle with the town folk, maybe knock down a few beers at a veterans hall or something like that. Sounded like a pretty good deal to most of us. Someone lied. Turned out most of us weren't old enough to drink.

We marched in the parade alright, with newly issued but mostly unfamiliar M-16s carried at sling arms. Instead of lingering in town afterward, we single filed right back onto the bus at the end of the parade route, stopped at an alcohol-free seafood restaurant for an early bird special of fried shrimp and clams, and returned dutifully to the fort where we proceeded to get some beers and party by ourselves. We could dress up your parade—whoever you are—and fight your war. But mingle? Heavens, no!

One More Track Meet

There was a battalion track meet one weekend. I went home instead. What was the point? First thing Monday morning I found myself standing at attention in front of our company commander, First Lieutenant Michael T. Ruane, who, many times before, had announced to the company that if we ever, ever stepped out of line our asses were grass and he was the lawn mower.

The last time he caught me going from Massachusetts to New Jersey on a 50-mile pass grass wasn't growing but, surprise, snow was falling. I shoveled it after supper for a week. He knew somehow I had been a runner. He chewed me out for technically having gone AWOL. He lived in Jersey City, less than ten miles from my home town, and those of us from Hudson County suspected he had gone "over the wall" himself a few times. So come on, Mike, give me a break. Curiously, he did; he gave me the rest of the week to get in shape for the all-post meet the coming Saturday. You might as well mow my ass right here and now, I thought to myself. Hurdlers are thoroughbreds. You can't just haul us around in a horse trailer, dump us at a track, and expect us to perform. It came down to this: the right way, the wrong way, or his way.

Not very much happens in the two or three city blocks that constitute Ayer, Massachusetts, the real world outside Fort Devens. But there was this track meet coming up and a local reporter discovered that there was a pretty good hurdler, New England champion of something or other, stationed right here at Fort Devens, a serious track man, it would seem, because this guy actually ran in his outfit's meet the week before. And won, easily. The paper ran a feature on him, action photo included.

So here's what happened. I show up at the track for practice Monday afternoon and this second lieutenant, the captain of our team it turns out, welcomes me. He asks what event I run and smiles broadly when I tell him I hurdle. "That's great," he said, because so did he. Not only that, he won the battalion 120-yard highs the week before while I was home probably drinking beer illegally. So, since he was team captain, and since he won the highs the week before, and since I was an unknown quantity to him, and since even if I was any good I had spent the better part of the past seven months or so doing jungle training in the snow not running, and since he didn't have anyone to run the 440-yard intermediate hurdles, I was the man. Welcome aboard!

Well, no, I told him. I don't run the quarter mile hurdles. I run the highs.

Now I had given Lieutenant I'm the Battalion Champion a case of the ass. After an attempt at pulling weight—not rank, mind you—he stormed away muttering something like, "We'll see about that." I spent the practice stretching and jogging and stretching, on the ground, on the hurdles, trying like hell not to pull a muscle. A few wind sprints, a couple of high steppers. More stretching. McHugh told me I'd never run again, and pulling a muscle going over the hurdles too hard after nearly two years away from them to impress this lewey would fulfill the prophecy. Military intelligence may have eluded me, but I knew something about hurdling and a little about my own body. One thing for sure: the quarter mile hurdles were out. Gas up the mower, Mike.

Something miraculous happened overnight. At Tuesday's practice, figuring raking up whatever would be left of my ass would consume the remainder of my week, Team Captain Lewey curtly tells me he entered me in the highs; he would run the 440 intermediates. God, I loved to run. More than that, I loved to run the high hurdles.

So here's what happened. I won the post championship on Saturday, beat the New England champ by a whole hurdle or more (no feature, no picture in the paper); I ran the lead-off leg on the 440-yard relay that also won; and scored in the triple jump, an event I had never competed in before. Ruane gave me a 50-mile pass. I went home.

Chapter 10

Leaving Home
June 1966

A simple child
That lightly draws its breath,
And feels its life in every limb,
What should it know of death?
William Wordsworth, *We Are Seven*

Pop insisted that we drive to the bus station in Newark alone, leaving Mom and the rest of the family's good-byes on Ann Street. A hug, a smile, a tear, a wave and we were gone. A light rain misted the windshield and I guess we commented on that. He wanted to talk, I thought at first, or maybe just to be alone together but we hardly spoke at all in the car.

Pop couldn't forget the scene from the night before, he couldn't say he was sorry either. He wasn't. Neither was I, although I was confused. I don't know when we lost control of the conversation, it just happened. I'm sorry now.

After dinner we had argued about war ... all wars, any war. At twenty, I was embarking for places I never heard of before, hostile places. Pop couldn't stop that. That disturbed him. He knew the horrors I was too naïve to imagine, but he was powerless to protect me from them. That frustrated him. I understand that now.

I blew up at Pop the last night of my last leave, loudly, very loudly, asserting my post-adolescent manhood. He deserved a son's respect; instead, he suffered my arrogance.

"I can take care of myself," I roared defiantly.

The tin words clanked against the shield of stubbornness which separated us. The volume of our voices camouflaged what we both truly felt, what I lacked the maturity to say.

Pop's anger was not with me, although it seemed so. He loved me too deeply to let me leave home, possibly never to return, harboring misconceptions of what war was all about. I wanted it to be a test, a personal challenge wreathed in glory and honor. He knew better. I know that now.

I ignored the fact that Pop was drafted into an earlier war to end all wars when he was already married and had two children. I was conceived on his last furlough before he embarked for the Pacific Theater, born while he was flushing Japanese guerrillas out of caves on Okinawa. Pop knew first hand the agony of separation, the fear that loneliness brings, and the vainglorious brutality men at war heap on one another. I am sorry he had to know.

Pop could not have been angry with me. Not then. He was angry with the world that lapsed again into senselessness, angry at the society that failed to resolve its differences peacefully. He was frustrated because his war did not prevent mine, did nothing to protect his son.

He insisted on driving me to Newark, just the two of us, for my return to Fort Devens. The 118 Public Service bus rounded the corner at Raymond Boulevard and nosed into the curb. Pop and I stepped back so that the other passengers could climb aboard, allowing ourselves a few extra, silent moments. We shook hands formally, then desperately threw our arms around each other and squeezed.

Pop's face pressed hard against my shoulder. "Take care of yourself," he ordered. "Take care of yourself." Thank God he didn't see the silent tears that flowed all the way up the New York State Throughway.

Chapter 11

Cruise Aboard the *General Alexander M. Patch*

July 1966

We'll o'er the water, we'll o'er the sea, / We'll o'er the water to Charlie;
Come weal, come woe, we'll gather and go, / And live and die wi' Charlie.

James Hogg, *O'er the Water to Charlie*

We knew we were going somewhere in July of '66: most likely Vietnam, maybe Santo Domingo. As usual, they weren't saying, so anywhere was possible. (Germany or Korea, perhaps? Nah!) Having returned from what we had been told for sure was our final stateside leave, all we had to do with our lives was prepare to ship out to wherever we were shipping out to. The Army made packing for the trip simple. They permitted all we could stuff into our back packs and those two duffel bags issued at Fort Dix.

Incidentally, one of the best arguments against Vietnam as a destination was the fact that the Army never issued us any clothing beyond our original allotment. No multi-hued, light weight jungle fatigues with deep external pockets on each side to replace industrial strength olive drab shirts and pants; no canvas-top jungle boots with steel-lined soles to protect against land mines or arch vents to promote air flow and facilitate drainage. We were no better outfitted for the jungle than we were for frozen tundra.

They assured us we were going somewhere, but they wouldn't tell us when. Soon, don't worry. For a couple of days, for the first time in our ten months stationed at Fort Devens, we had nothing to do. They made us clean the barracks, of course, but that didn't take long. Then typical Army harassment began with random roll calls—morning, noon, and night. Whenever roll call sounded, we had to fall out of the barracks and into formation on the battalion quadrangle, on the double, ready to deploy to wherever it was we were going, with all our worldly possessions: weapon, steel pot, pistol belt and harness, backpack, and two stuffed duffel bags. Oh, and by the way, we had to leave our bunks with blankets folded and stacked neatly on the mattress which had to be rolled into an "S" at the head of the bunk, or was it the foot? (Who the hell was going to check, and what would they do if someone defied that chicken shit order anyway?)

At every formation, our company commander, or his executive officer, put himself on the line to the battalion commander, or his executive officer, when he barked, "Company A all present or accounted for, Sir." This meant he knew the exact whereabouts of all his men, even if one was not actually in formation— sick call, perhaps, or some other "accounted for" location. Anyone unaccounted for was AWOL which, given our readiness for overseas deployment, would render that person technically a deserter. Random roll calls amounted to just another pain in the ass for the troops. For the hierarchy of officers reporting up the line, however, it meant verbal assurance that the brigade would be at full strength when we finally did ship out to wherever it was we were shipping out to. At last, the final muster and roll call came.

We had gotten used to hearing commanders of A, B, C, and D companies yell out one after the other, "All present or accounted for, Sir." The battalion commander would then yell back something like, "Company commanders, take charge of your troops." Ruane usually admonished us about not leaving the company area with an expressed or implied "your ass is grass" comment and then dismiss us. The morning of the final muster went something like this:

"Company A all present or accounted for, Sir."

"Company B all present or accounted for, Sir."

"Company C all present or accounted for, Sir."

"Company D all present or accounted for, Sir."

While we assembled in the morning sun, a caravan of commercial buses lined up on the street—real buses with seats and storage compartments this time, not horse trailers. The battalion commander read from a sheet of paper that turned out to be our orders. "Gobbledegook, gobbledegook, high falutin' gobbledegook," he read in monotone, "More gobbledegook, blah, blah, blah, port of call, Vung Tau, Republic of South Vietnam." No moaning or groaning, jeering or cheering. We filed onto the buses which proceeded directly to Boston Harbor.

Welcome Aboard

The Merchant Marine troop ship, *General Alexander M. Patch*, snuggled up to the dock in tandem with a sister ship awaiting our arrival. The scene might have resembled one of those old war movies where all the dearly beloved gather together to see their soldier boys off on their way to conquer evil. This scene, you know the one: waving arms, blowing kisses, smiling oh-so-brave-upper-lipishly, and running up and down the pier trying desperately to make eye contact one last time and form "I love you" on ruby red lips (in black and white).

It might have been like that, but it wasn't. Until that morning, we didn't know where we were going, when we were going, or how we were going to get wherever it was we were going. At Fort Devens, we were already soldiers away from home and had managed private goodbyes some time before.

Revenge of the Duffel Bags

The symbolic act of crossing the gang plank from shore to ship carried with it an existential sense of separation of heart and body. Would these feet ever again alight upon American ground? Would this heart ever leave it?

We knew going in that this was not going to be a leisurely summer cruise down the Atlantic coast, through the Panama Canal, up to San Diego for refueling, and all the way across the Pacific to the South China Sea. No way.

Once aboard the *General Alexander M. Patch*, they let us know right away that, Ultimate Weapons or not, we were pretty much cargo. ("They" no longer meant just nameless, faceless, high ranking Army guys, but now included Navy officers, because we carried weapons and ammunition aboard, and Merchant Marine officers and crew, because it was their ship.) The newly conglomerated "they" proved up to the task of exercising control over us and our miserable, grassy-assed lives. They did this the old fashioned way. They continually found innovative ways to piss us off.

Welcome aboard. Keep moving, keep moving. You there, come on, come on, hurry up, yeah you. Down those stairs to the deck below. Keep going. Down, down. Next deck. Around that corner, down another flight. No more decks. Down. No more stairs. Through that bulkhead (nautical talk for wall). Pick a bunk. Say hello to your home for the next month.

Make the most of it. Improvise. This could resemble home, I rationalized, because I got the top bunk again. But where do I stow my stuff, you know, my duffel bags? Go down that-a-way, between those rows of double-decker bunks that you can't see the end of now but you will when you get there, then take a right and go down that lane for awhile, then a left when you see an overhead light at starboard, and you can't miss the storage area. Starboard? At the end of that maze, an empty room lay interred in the stuffy womb of the ship. I placed my duffel bags neatly near the several others already there.

In short order, duffel bags mated with other duffel bags and those duffel bags mated with more duffel bags until a mound of cloned duffel bags ten feet high filled the room. Need to change your boxers? No problem. Find your duffel bag, the one with the underwear and socks not the one with the fatigues that weathered you through the New England winter. Pissed off, who's pissed off? You ain't gonna piss me off with that little hide and go seek the duffel bag trick.

Two or three days out of Boston, the anonymous social director for the voyage announced plans for a mustache growing contest. What a great idea. When not immersed in the daily elbow-wielding burrowing through Mount Duffel in search of reasonably hygienic drawers, we could cultivate facial hair, walk those unrestricted sections of the ship—home away from home—find a mirror to check hourly progress. What great fun. Now we have something to do. On the approach to San Diego, he, whoever he was, canceled the contest. Everybody shave. Can't pull into a naval base looking like a bunch of post-adolescent rag-a-muffins in front of all those sailors, and the picture on your military ID doesn't show a mustache so that fuzz above your lip is illegal anyway.

Everybody shaved. Two or three days out of San Diego the social director announced plans for a mustache growing contest. What a great idea. Now we have something to do. On the approach to Vung Tau two weeks later, he canceled the contest. Everybody shave. Can't pull into a combat zone looking like a bunch of post-adolescent rag-a-muffins in front of all those . . . all those . . . all those, oh you know what I mean, and the picture on your military ID doesn't show a mustache so that fuzz above your lip is illegal anyway.

Travelogue

Under different circumstances, this would have been one hell of an ocean voyage. South of the Carolinas the Atlantic appeared cleaner, deeper, bluer. Every now and then schools of flying fish escorted the *Patch*. They seemed to enjoy the race, maintaining the same pace, but staying just ahead of us. God, what a beautiful sight.

The voyage would eventually lead us below the equator and back. Seafaring folk make a fuss over this, some sort of right of passage for a sailor, I guess. For those of us traveling steerage, however, crossing the equator merely meant another nautical mile closer to Vietnam. And for some it meant sun poisoning, a serious matter for light infantrymen who would soon be expected to carry heavy loads on their backs into battle. Just as the Army didn't issue us jungle fatigues or jungle boots even though we were headed for the jungle, neither did they issue sun screen even though we were headed directly for the stretch of globe where Father Sun is closest to Mother Earth. Sunburn for many, sun poison for a few. Because of this, before we left the Atlantic Ocean, an order was issued making it a punishable offense, under Article 15,[10] for anyone to be caught shirtless on deck. For Caucasians, cosmetic coloring from the cruise would be limited to a farmer's tan, at best; for me, it didn't matter, because I don't tan anyway.

Then there was Panama. We sat outside the canal for two days or so—shirts could be rolled up to the elbow during the day—awaiting our turn through the locks. While literally being pulled through the canal, to the north at Colon, I remember a gorgeous waterfall. To the south, American tanks pointed their turrets away from the virtually dry docked ship, for protection we were told. When Russian ships passed through the canal, the guns pointed at them. I couldn't imagine then what we were being protected from, but nonetheless being pulled through the locks, flooded then emptied, did produce a feeling of vulnerability. We were out of place. We were literally on a ship out of water, sunburned transient Caribbean travelers dressed in heavy, long pants and heavy, long-sleeve shirts.

The Navy Gets the Gravy

Having passed through the canal without event—no pop-gun-toting guerrillas dumb enough to challenge tank-mounted cannons—we proceeded north along the coast to the San Diego Naval Base for refueling, a two-day layover. Oops! Here comes that military intelligence thing again: two troop ships teeming with a couple thousand alcohol-deprived, hormone-enriched young bucks, destined for who-knew-what, about to set foot on the last American soil they would see in a year, if they were to return at all. Sunburned soldiers with pale upper lips because they had to shave before they were allowed to be seen by sailors their own age, soldiers the age of draft-dodging college students, soldiers who had to go on a major tunneling expedition through hostile duffel bag territory every day just to dig out a clean pair of boxers, soldiers who quite simply had absolutely nothing to lose, were about to be let loose for pre-combat rest and relaxation in balmy southern California.

So here's what happened. Bobby Fisher, Willie Bonds, Bob Fauvre, and I somehow make our way to an enlisted man's club which, wonder of wonders, was packed tighter than the horse trailers at Fort Dix. We huddled outside for a minute and devised a plan: whoever made it to the bar first would get a case of beer, signal the others, and we'd meet at one of the trees in the grassy strip just across the sidewalk in front of the club. Having negotiated Duffel Bag Mountain every day for the previous two weeks proved great training for wending one's way to the bar. Fauvre, I think, secured the liquid gold. In short order, four buddies from Jersey wearing "shit eatin' grins"[11] (Platoon Sergeant Griffin's frequently used terminology) propped ourselves up against a palm tree, armed with a cool six pack apiece to fend off the parching effects of the warm California sun.

Less than two beers into our private party, bodies start flying out of the club. Then a stool comes through the picture window. Then the whistles blow and sailor cops with billy clubs appear from nowhere. Shit eatin' grins gave way to rollicking laughter for the spectators from New Jersey who almost any other day would have found themselves right in the middle of the melee. It was almost like an out of body experience watching others who were so much like ourselves getting hauled out of a bar. We finished our beers.

Lock and Load

Did I mention that they took away the M-14 rifles we had trained and qualified on (Marksman, Sharpshooter, or Expert) and replaced them with Congress's latest pork barrel tribute to mass-produced weaponry, the M-16? Those of us who carried a rifle, which was most of us seeing that we were in a rifle platoon in a rifle company in an infantry brigade, were on our way, the Army way, into combat with a weapon we never fired. Not a single round. Not to worry.

Somewhere squeezed into our busy mustache growing schedules they brought squads of us to a formerly restricted area of the ship, the fantail—the back, the after part—more accurately described as the rear end of the ship because from there, we learned, GIs on KP dumped kitchen waste into the Pacific Ocean. That's right. General Patch shit tons of garbage from Southern California to Southeast Asia. What a guy. But I digress.

Sailing along the high sea, military intelligence or Yankee ingenuity or a bolt of lightning or something struck someone in the grey matter. He, whoever he was, figured that God had created the ultimate firing range for the Ultimate Weapons to fire the latest ultimate weapon. He called a special meeting in the officer's mess for all land lubbing pooh-bahs, I can picture them now, and together 'round a steaming hot pot of Jo they concocted a plan devised to acquaint us with our rifles. God, they were good.

With us lined along the rear-most edge of the ship, M-16s in hand, they issued each of us a magazine of bullets (twenty or less) with no fear of anyone accidentally wandering in front of the firing line. The range extended literally from the rail of the ship to the horizon. Sergeant Somebody assumed command.

"The firing line is clear.

"Second Squad: Lock and load your weapons.

"KP Detail: Ready. Lift your cans. Toss your garbage.

"Squad: Ready. Aim. Fire at will."

The M-16 didn't feel like, sound like, or act like the M-14. It was shorter, lighter, and the stock was made of plastic, for God's sake. Also unlike the M-14, every M-16 had a selector switch that made every weapon fully automatic (hold the trigger back and bullets keep flying). While this might seem like a good idea, in reality it is not because the tendency for an undisciplined rifleman under the stress of a fire fight is to take too many random shots, usually at a guesstimated target. At least three problems arise when this happens: first, the shooter empties his magazine in one or two squeezes which renders him and his buddies vulnerable to hostile fire because he has to stop to replace the magazine; second, firing so rapidly tends to overheat—and therefore expand—the chamber which causes jams because the cartridge cannot eject; and third, a rifle squad has two designated automatic riflemen, trained specifically to lay down a base of fire while their buddies carry out their assignments virtually by rote—when anyone, or everyone, attacks in the same way, learned tactics are lost. The point here is that firing live ammunition for the first time, even at garbage, gives a certain thrill; firing faster, some might think, gives a bigger thrill and so some of us flipped the switch and fired away. Bottom line: we got to fire our weapons, which of course was important, but we weren't firing for effect, we weren't zeroing them in.

"Cease fire.

"Lock and clear your weapons."

Having fired our weapons in the salty sea air, we now had something else to do besides growing our mustaches; we got to clean our rifles. In truth, in this regard the M-16 held a distinct advantage over the M-14. It was very easy to disassemble, and therefore to clean. But guess where our rifle cleaning stuff was stashed. Mount Duffel.

Chapter 12

Hello, Vietnam
August 1966

They were going to look at war, the red animal war, the blood-swollen god.

Stephen Crane, *The Red Badge of Courage*

Not much else happened during the two week cruise between southern California and Southeast Asia. An amateurish newsletter appeared every couple of days from "Davey Jones's Locker," a character I guess who carries symbolic meaning for seafaring men. I remember reading how something big was supposed to occur when we crossed the international date line, but nothing did. All I remember about the passage of time was resetting my Timex every time we passed into another time zone. Finally, we arrived.

The Patch sat off the coast of Vietnam for two nights. We saw occasional flashes of light and heard for the first time the sounds of war we would hear again and again for the duration of our tour. I don't remember being scared, although I must have been. I just remember a heightened perception of sensual awareness and thinking about how recognizing sights and sounds might save my life.

After two nights watching the intermittent fireworks, the 196th Light Infantry Brigade prepared to hit the beach—in full battle gear, weapons slung over our shoulders, and carrying two freaking duffel bags apiece.

The Patch disgorged us at sea level and spit us across a gangplank onto landing craft. "Jesus Christ," I thought while huddled duffel bag to duffel bag in a great big tub whose walls were too high to see over, "I hope we don't get pinned down in the water or on the beach; not now, not the first freaking day, not carrying dirty socks and underwear in these two freaking duffel bags." Not to worry. Our boat dropped its forward wall to let us disembark into the shallow water. Then, unbelievably, as we waded out of the South China Sea, children greeted us with leis while a small band played I-don't-have-a-clue-what because I was so stunned. The night before ... no, this couldn't be the same place. The ship must have sailed to another port of call while we slept.

As it turned out, Vung Tau was a safe spot. In fact, it had been a fancy resort in happier times, the Paris of the Orient. And it was considered so secure that American soldiers used it as an in-country R&R location during most of the war. This is Vietnam? This is war? This can't be. Right. It can't. It wasn't.

We sloshed our way through the children without stopping and loaded directly onto waiting deuce-and-a-halfs (2 ½ ton trucks) that immediately took us to a nearby airfield. Apparently our steerage class tickets on the Patch easily transferred to similar accommodations on the air transports. Yup, duffel bag to duffel bag in the middle of a cargo plane. We didn't have to worry about returning our trays to an upright position or even fastening our seat belts for that matter. But, you know what, sitting on a couple of duffel bags beats the hell out of squeezing into a cabin class airplane seat whose cushion can be used as a flotation device anyway. Final destination: Tay Ninh.

Tay Ninh, Ant Hills, and a Scorpion

Tay Ninh is a city within a province of the same name located almost directly west of Saigon and just a few miles east of the Cambodian border. Vung Tau it was not. We landed on a makeshift runway. Tanks had formed a perimeter and served as our primary defense against who knew what for the first few days. Our first job was to establish a base camp, starting with sand-bag bunkers to replace the tanks, then tent erection to provide shelter from the tropical sun for us and, coincidentally, bulls eyes for VC mortar men in the moonlight.

It took me years to tell the story about building the base camp, because even to me it sounded like a lie. Mounds, some as much as six feet high, littered the terrain allocated to us as home. (An old joke said that the mosquitoes were so big in Vietnam that once, when one set down on an air strip, ground personnel refueled it.) Well these mounds were no joke, they were anthills, and they had to come down. No easy task. The sun-baked mud walls bent our shovels and scoffed at attempts to penetrate them with pickaxes. Not to be daunted by a bunch of ants who had probably taken a millennium to construct their tropical bungalows, we blew them up. We scattered billions of mean spirited ants across our newly acquired real estate. I can't imagine that this amused them. Not only that, it turns out the ants shared their fortresses with other creatures, unbeknown to us North American invaders, of course. Demolishing anthills, nonetheless, became great fun. Boom! Boom! Baboom!

Then a strange thing happened. "Fire in the hole," somebody shouted to alert the rest of us that the C-4 was in place and he was about to level another hill. We took cover. Boom! Shards of mud and countless pissed off ants floated to the ground. When the dust settled on the sight where the anthill had been, we saw an almost phosphorescent green snake slithering aimlessly. Someone said it was a cobra. Maybe. Could have been a boa constrictor or an electric eel for all I knew; "snake" was enough for me not to go anywhere near it. A couple of the braver, or dumber, guys began to taunt it with their shovels until a voice of authority warned that snakes don't travel alone. Now, how would anyone know that, I thought. Seconds later two more appeared, smaller and a lighter shade of shimmering green.

As much as I hate snakes (I don't care whether they're slimy or not, they make me cringe), there was an awesome beauty to these creatures. And I couldn't help but think how incredible it was that they were living inside a natural structure, which they built, that required explosives to penetrate. If the ants and snakes were this tough, what must the Viet Cong be like?

Having evicted the previous squatters, we began to settle in. One evening during my first week in country, I was sitting on a row of sandbags we had laid around our tent as protection against mortar attack. I sat with left hand flat atop the row, fingers pointed away from my body, with my head turned to the right, facing a buddy with whom I was talking about nothing in particular. Mosquitoes and ants, probably. I turned for no particular reason to the left just in time to see a scorpion, his ugly face almost touching my middle finger, poised to strike. Before I could move, he whipped his tail over his body and struck the back of my hand which almost immediately swelled to the size of a catcher's mitt.

"Oh, man, that's too bad," the medic in the first aid tent half moaned, half-sighed. "What? What?" "It's your left hand. If that bastard had stung you on the other hand, you know, with the trigger finger, we'd have had to send you home."

In less than one week, before I engaged my first VC, I had encountered warrior ants, snakes, and a scorpion. Welcome to Vietnam. I was ready to stow away on the next mosquito out of there.

Sitting in altar boy cassock,
circa 1957–58, about the
time of Confirmation.

Tom Nash, Paul Drew (app. 180 lbs.), Bob Fisher en route to
Vietnam aboard the *General Alexander M. Patch*, somewhere
on the Pacific Ocean, August 1966.

Members of the 2nd Platoon, A. Co., 3rd Bn., 21st Inf, 196th Light Infantry Brigade, relaxing at their Cu Chi base camp, circa 1967. Front row left to right: Jones, Nelson, Flores, Mashburn, Salerno, Conley; second row: Drew, Aytch, Hunt, Nobles, Lomax, Craig.

Waiting for helicopter transport to base camp. Paul Drew in center, leaning on left elbow; King to his right; standing Bob Fauvre and Lanny Wadkins; Willie Lomax standing far right with head turned; Lowell Garland sitting far right.

Mom's homemade greeting.

At the dinner table, first night home. Paul (app. 160 lbs.), Dad, and brother Paschal.

Family men, 1972. Left to right: Paul; father, Charles; brothers, Paschal and Charles; brother-in-law, Paul Heaney.

Paul and cousin, Dennis Russell, days before the author returned home, July 1967.

Teaching, circa 1970–71.

Part III

Combat Infantry
1966–67

Chapter 13

Nui Ba Denh, Black Virgin Mountain

What use bombs and antibombs,
Sovereign powers, brutal lives, ugly deaths?
Are men born to go down like this?
Jean Toomer, *The Blue Meridian*

War may be hell, as Union General William Tecumseh Sherman put it when recalling personal experiences and observations during the Civil War, but often the pre-battle field is beautiful. Any GI who served in War Zone C will never forget the magnificence of Nui Ba Denh, Black Virgin Mountain, ascending majestically toward the sky out of the sanctuary of the deserted Michelin Rubber Plantation. This virgin, however, had long before relinquished her chastity to the Viet Cong who regularly sought refuge beneath her verdant petticoats. Nature's artistry and man's defoliation of her handiwork converged at Nui Ba Denh.

Not long into our tour, two weeks, perhaps, we loaded into a caravan of deuce-and-a-halfs which trucked us from our not-yet-complete base camp near Tay Ninh City out to the base of the mountain. Once we established a hasty defensive perimeter, we set up makeshift targets with the mountain as backstop so that we could at last zero our M-16s. Before everyone got a turn to accomplish this important calibration on the weapon we would depend upon, literally, for our lives, however, a helicopter crashed into the mountain. No longer a leisurely trip to a shooting gallery in the woods, circumstances had dictated our first combat mission: search for and recover all who had been aboard.

We didn't know at the time how the helicopter came to crash. Was it shot down? If so, from where and with what kind of weapon? We didn't know how many people it carried, where their flight originated, or what their mission was. Although there was no hesitation or question that we had to get to the crash site as quickly as possible, we simply had no idea what we would encounter along the way.

There may have been footpaths hidden somewhere beneath the jungle canopy that bedecked Nui Ba Denh, but we had no clue where they were; and even if we did, the VC probably had booby trapped them. We lined up Indian file and climbed the mountain serpentine. I remember vividly taking turns helping each other scale the escarpments: cupping hands to boost a buddy upward, hanging down to pull another up—for hours. We reached the crash site just before dark—without enemy encounter—and found four burned-beyond-recognition bodies amid the metallic rubble. Welcome to Death.

Welcome to war. Real war. Not war games, not Hollywood war. Before ever even seeing a single enemy soldier, much less firing a bullet in his direction, we met Death, the most devastating and inevitable product of war, in the persons of four hideously charred Americans we didn't know and couldn't recognize even if we did.

With no rations, because we hadn't planned on camping out for the night, and less than a combat load of ammunition per man for the same reason, we spent a frightening night on that mountain. Even if we had packed entrenching tools (Armyspeak for fold-up shovels) to dig foxholes, we would not have been able to penetrate the rock. All that silly-ass training in the snow went for naught that night on Nui Ba Denh, I thought.

Intermittent man-made explosions interrupted Nature's night sounds. All night. Maybe it was us bombing them, maybe them bombing us. It didn't really matter. The ugly face of war had stolen the beauty of Nui Ba Denh and, that day, ravaged any romantic notions that virgin soldiers have about war. This wasn't training anymore. It wasn't an academic symposium. Real people died in that crash on Nui Ba Denh, and this real person experienced, for the first time in his young life real fear. And real sorrow for the abbreviated lives of people I did not know.

When daylight finally, mercifully, came, we had to carry the bodies down the mountain. The first squad—I think it was the first squad—wrapped the remains in ponchos and we, the second squad, served as pall bearers. Just as we had employed the buddy system to reach the crash site the day before, now we had to reverse the process with the added awesome responsibility of passing what remained of someone's son or husband down the rocks.

"Do not weep, Maiden. / War is kind" Stephen Crane wrote sarcastically. Casualties of war—any war, every war—should cause the whole world to weep.

At one point I was the bottom man, having slid down a big rock first. Two guys eased the body, nearly vertical, toward me. I would support the weight and wait for one of them to lower himself to where I was standing and together we would ease the corpse to our level and then repeat the process as many times as necessary.

How much does an incinerated adult weigh? A thousand pounds. More. I didn't know whether my hands had grasped feet or shoulders on the inside of the slick shroud. But looking up I saw that a fractured bone from an indistinguishable body part had pierced through the rubber, and brown liquid was dripping onto me from somewhere. There was a smell not unlike burnt chicken, and flies swarmed and jostled each other for landing spots on the protruding splinters. That body weighed a ton, and I couldn't lower it without help. I knew intuitively that I dare not desecrate it by dropping it or letting it slip. The circumstance of war had already defiled him—or her. At that very early point in my combat tour I understood the precariousness of life, all life, in a war zone.

Remember, Paul, that you are dust. How can I ever forget?

At virtually the same time, McNamara, with wife and friends, were also mountain climbing. It seems the Secretary of Defense needed to escape the pressure cooker atmosphere of Washington, D.C. where he had been subjected to the cacophony of the anti-war movement. He writes, "My encounters with ... protests became louder and uglier. One of the more disturbing was in August 1966. My family and I were waiting to board a plane at Seattle airport after having climbed Mount Rainier with Jim and Lou Whittaker (Jim was the first American to Conquer Mount Everest). A man approached, shouted 'Murderer!' and spat on me." McNamara managed to escape again in December. He recalls: "Then, during the Christmas holidays, while I was lunching with Marg at a restaurant on top of Aspen Mountain, a woman came to the table and in a voice loud enough to be heard across the room, screamed, 'Baby burner! You have blood on your hands!'" (*IR*, 258). "Some nights in 1967," McNamara confesses, "I had to take a pill in order to sleep" (*IR*, 260).

I'm sorry for your discomfort, Sir; but to be honest I'm happy to hear that some agonizing occurred. I have to tell you, though, the Army didn't issue us sleeping pills in Vietnam along with our daily dose of quinine to ward off malaria. Some nights for me in 1966–67, in the relative luxury of base camp, I got myself shit-faced with alcohol in order to sleep. The demons I faced on Nui Ba Denh would have devoured those you sought to conquer on Mount Ranier. I'm sorry for your discomfort, but I'm not participating in your pity party.

Chapter 14

Pulling the Pin

The ceremony of innocence is drowned.
William Butler Yeats, *The Second Coming*

Not long after our first encounter with Death on Nui Ba Denh, the platoon went out on patrol in a free-fire zone (designated as enemy held; all indigenous personnel suspected to be Viet Cong or VC sympathizers). The area wasn't quite as lush as the Michelin Rubber Plantation sprawled at the foot of the Black Virgin, but it wasn't dense jungle either. In fact, we found the terrain relatively easy to navigate, and, because visibility was also good, we traversed the area in box formation (that is, the second squad—mine—stretched out across the front, and the other squads in the platoon positioned along the sides and the rear with the platoon leader, platoon sergeant, radio operator, and medic floating in no particular pattern within the perimeter).

We saw a small clearing ahead, I'm guessing, maybe fifty yards by fifty yards. We halted the patrol in order to decide how best to negotiate this open space. Plunging straight ahead could be suicide for the squad. Breaking formation and proceeding single file to one side or the other would sacrifice flank security and possibly throw us off our azimuth. The plan came down that the squads on either flank would skirt the edges of the wood line, thereby establishing some lateral security, and the second squad would advance cautiously across the open stretch: run a few steps one fire team at a time, hit the dirt, run a few steps, hit the dirt until we reached the other side.

As we dropped to the ground maybe twenty yards or so into the clearing, I saw a flash of movement behind a pile of dirt at the far left corner, that is, at the beginning of the woods we were headed toward. The mound itself looked suspicious because it appeared from the color of the dirt to be freshly dug. A bunker, perhaps; a foxhole; a grave?

Without much thought, I signaled to the rest of the squad and both flanks to stay down. Then I detached a hand grenade from my harness and low crawled directly toward the target. When I got close enough to feel comfortable that I could lob the grenade just over the berm thereby causing maximum destruction to whomever or whatever lay behind it, I pulled the pin, tossed the grenade, and still on my belly tried to squeeze my entire body inside my steel pot for protection, in case the shrapnel blew through or over the mound. Bulls eye. The throw was perfect but the explosion less than expected, since without thinking about it I had selected a concussion grenade—designed to wreak its havoc in tunnels—not a fragmentation grenade, loaded with metal shards—designed to shred human flesh. I now had to inspect the result of my first deliberate belligerent act.

I'm not sure what I expected. But having already experienced the horror at Nui Ba Denh, I knew it would be ugly. Dismemberment at the very least, I figured, as I followed the point of my M-16 around the side of the mound, prepared to pull the trigger if necessary to complete my gruesome task. I found nothing. No body. No body parts. Nothing. If in fact the movement I saw was a person, and now I couldn't be sure that it wasn't another of God's creatures, that person managed to retreat unnoticed through the woods and escape death at my hands.

Over the years, as I have remembered and thought sometimes very deeply about this incident, I feel alternately blessed and damned. I'm glad that a person did not die that day even though part of me did. For I knew from that instant what I am capable of. Without emotion, without hesitation, with no sense of guilt at the moment, I could kill. I could kill someone I never met and didn't hate. My innocence lay shattered in the dirt that day.

"Tyger, Tyger ... Did He Who made the Lamb make Thee?"
WILLIAM BLAKE

I have read about just wars and good wars, self defense, and justifiable homicide. I have heard people say that they could and would do anything necessary to preserve their own lives, and that soldiers should never be asked to second guess their actions on the battlefield. I have also heard people proclaim self-righteously that under no circumstances could they or would they take another's life. Words, mere words. Ignorance passing itself off as innocence. Sophistry, not philosophy.

A paradox of war is that, within the context of this basest of human activities, individuals often discover in themselves and others the highest of human qualities: patriotism, honor, loyalty, courage, comradeship, dignity, love of life. The moment I pulled that pin, however, I discovered the nadir of my humanness. And from that moment I forfeited forever the luxury of philosophizing about war.

Chapter 15

One for the Dogs

What! Must I hold a candle to my shames?

Shakespeare, *Merchant of Venice*

Ambush is tricky business. If not extremely careful in setting an ambush, ambushers become ambushees. The second squad left base camp about dusk, headed for the staging area from where we would snake silently into the night. This night the squad was reinforced with a machine gun crew and a special guest, a German Shepherd.

We patrolled without incident to our destination and slipped into place at the edge of a wood line. Alpha Team settled in on the right, Bravo on the left, with the machine gun crew, the dog, and me in the corner. We positioned ourselves such that we had bright, moonlit rice paddies in front and to the left. As far as we could see, sparse woods shaded a few hootches and livestock pens to the right. The setup was superb. Because we occupied a corner, we enjoyed flank security on both sides. We could see clearly in front for several hundred yards, and the jungle itself protected our rear.

You should have seen the dog. What a magnificent animal. He sat regally, sphinx-like, hind legs under him with paws flat and pointed straight out, front legs fully extended from shoulders to the ground. He never made a noise of any kind, yet somehow knew how to distinguish jungle sounds. He looked straight ahead most of the time. At the sound of movement not indigenous to the jungle, maybe a restless soldier's boot, he turned his snout directly at the suspicious noise, still making no sound of his own.

Click. The strike of a match. Before the flicker appeared in the vicinity of the hootches, the shepherd snapped his head toward it, ears standing at attention. This signaled the alert to all of us that something was happening. The light moved slowly toward the rice paddy about thirty-five or forty yards down range. This offered a rare opportunity for the combat infantryman to actually take proper aim at a human target from the prone position.

The second squad was well disciplined. Adrenaline raced through our veins—mine for sure—but nobody moved, everyone waiting for my signal to open fire. To shoot at first sight would have been stupid because then we would never know how many bad guys were in the party or what sort of weapons they had. Plus, we would give away our own position prematurely. We needed to wait until more of them appeared or until he, or they, turned toward us thereby presenting a threat. God, we were ready. If there was such a thing as a perfect ambush, this was it.

The guy kept walking slowly in front of us, right to left. He carried a small lantern. He walked gingerly into the rice paddy, kind of sloshing because of the irrigation. Didn't look like he was carrying a weapon. That didn't matter. Maybe he was armed under the black pajamas. Maybe he had grenades strapped to his body. Maybe he was going to plant a mine or two. Whatever. We were ready for him.

He kept walking until he was just about dead center with the barrel of the machine gun. It doesn't get any better than that. Still alone. He stooped to place the lantern down. With a deftness that comes only with years of practice, in a single motion his pajamas dropped to his ankles and he squatted. Elbows on knees, hands under chin, he relieves himself in front of the second squad, a machine gun crew, and a stone-faced dog.

My guess is that he knew we were there all along and figured that if he made noise back in the hootch area he might draw our fire. Incidents like this demonstrate the restraint American soldiers exercised more often than people tend to believe. We had no reason to spring the ambush that night, and so we didn't. No one got trigger happy. No one forgot or ignored the order issued hours before to hold fire until I gave the command.

As for the squatter, he simply acted out the adage, it's better to bear the shame than bear the pain. He re-covered the second moon shining that night and shuffled himself back to where his buffalo roamed.

Chapter 16

Cheating Death

Death be not proud, though some have called thee
Mighty and dreadful, for thou art not so,
For those whom thou thinks'st thou dost overthrow,
Die not, poor death, nor yet canst thou kill me.

John Donne, *Hymn to Christ*

Although, of all people in the world, combat soldiers know they are not invincible, often, paradoxically, they have to act as though they believe that they are in order to survive. For example, a lesson learned somewhere in the Pine Tree Jungle of the Great American Northeast: The only way out of an ambush, Sergeant Griffin taught us, is to attack its strongest point. "If you are pinned down and you stay down, you'll never get up to talk about it." As usual, we took this World War II and Korean War veteran's word as gospel. (This particular Griffinism was not to be confused with his "when you're on line, don't run out in front or you'll become a 'flopper'" dictum.)

During a situational training exercise back in the states, we encountered an enemy machine gun position, while cadre walked around the battlefield determining who had been killed. When the concealed enemy opened fire on us, I was about fifteen or twenty yards down range and maybe 45 degrees or so off center.

I dove safely behind a tree trunk as the gunner laid down a base of fire left to right and back again. Missed me, sucker. Anticipating his firing motion, I bolted to another tree, maybe five yards or so closer to the gun, as he sprayed in the other direction.

Tap, tap on the helmet. "You just ran in front of a machine gun, son. You can't do that." I hadn't, really; in fact I had actually secured a position from which I could have knocked out the nest with a hand grenade. "You're dead." I could have been a hero, but this demigod had declared me dead. Son of a bitch!

I'm not sure what lesson, if any, I learned that day. "Don't run in front of a machine gun" doesn't seem like something that needed to be taught. "Hide behind a tree until the bad guys run out of ammunition" doesn't seem quite right, either. "Most heroes die while committing a courageous act" could be close.

So here's what happened for real.

Alpha Company, 3rd Battalion, 21st Infantry got called out early in the morning. For once, we had some intelligence. We were going on a company size mission into hostile territory. We were going somewhere where we would need to dig in. And, by the way, the LZ (landing zone) would likely be hot. Supply issued us a few long handled shovels and other miscellaneous gardening tools that we would be required to carry in duffel bags along with all the other shit that made us "light."

When we arrived at the helicopter pickup point, second platoon got the order to hop on the first sortie. Second squad loaded into the third and fourth birds. Lowell Garland (Indiana) and I were the team leaders at the time. We'd been together since the beginning at Devens and actually shared a room after basic training when we were made acting jacks as team leaders.

Not sure how it happened, but Lowell and I came to respect each other. And even though he tended to hang with Hoosiers while I with Garden Staters in the off hours, respect turned to genuine friendship and finally to total trust. In the jungle there was never a question that his team—and later his squad—would be exactly where they should be. Reliable doesn't sound like a very strong world. But let me tell you, patrolling the jungle is a trust walk. You have to trust that the other good guys are where they are supposed to be—flank security, for example. So reliable also means predictable, and Lowell was all of that.

With that as backdrop, we loaded our teams into the choppers. I hopped up last so that I was sitting next to the machine gunner, facing out. This would allow me to jump out first to group and position my team, not knowing of course from what direction we might take fire and therefore where we would have to attack. (Quick recap: We're in the first sortie, carrying shovels and duffel bags full of digging in shit, expecting to engage the enemy. Yup, Army intelligence.)

We got hit hard. As the sorties hovered down into what appeared on the map as a clearing but turned out to be elephant grass, Charlie opened up. They had turned at least one Chinese antitank mine upside down and detonated it in front of our Huey. Most of the machine gun fire was coming from a nest just inside the wood line, almost directly in front of me. The helicopter crew screamed for us to jump out. We had no choice, really. We couldn't stay, and they had to get their sitting duck asses out of there.

Bill Soyk, Wisconsin, was sitting in the middle. Although a big, rugged guy, he was one of the gentlest, nicest people I have ever met. He didn't smoke, drink, or curse; didn't go to the movies, for God's sake. He also didn't complain about those of us who did smoke, drink, curse, and carry on. He was a good person and a good soldier. Sitting in the middle of the chopper he took a bullet through the neck.

We bailed out of that bird like it had leprosy. We were in deep shit but nobody panicked. In no time, Alpha Team was spread out alongside each other firing into the wood line, just the way Griffin had drilled us, and there was Lowell and Bravo doing the same. And there was Bill Soyk, lying on the ground right behind me. I have no idea how he got there. Did he jump instinctively? Did one of those son-of-a-bitching machine gunners push him out? All I remember is pressing my hand against his neck to stop the bleeding. Private King, a rifleman who had joined the brigade as a replacement, was right there and he replaced my hand with his and stayed with Bill. I never saw Bill Soyk again.

Bullets sprayed so freely on both sides that they actually mowed the grass. The second squad performed magnificently. Alpha Team got up and charged a few steps, while Bravo laid down a base of fire. Vice versa. In the middle of one charge, a VC grenade exploded a few yards away just as we dive to the ground. Shrapnel flew over our heads. Willie Bonds was pumping grenades into the wood line from his M-79. Fisher, Fauvre. Everybody was firing, advancing, staying on line. Attack the ambush, Griffin had taught us, or you'll never live to talk about it.

Trust me on this one. In this situation, there is no such thing as squinting down the barrel of your rifle, drawing a bead on a bad guy's chest, and popping off a round or two. You point at where most of the noise is coming from, pull the trigger and hope. Hope you hit him before he hits you. Not having ever actually zeroed my M-16, at one point during this melee while I lay prone, I fired a whole magazine at a tree. I couldn't see Charlie but I could see the tree, and I intended to watch my tracers.

The good news was I hit the tree. But firing a whole magazine overheated the chamber and the last case wouldn't eject. I loaded a new magazine and when we charged again I banged the rifle butt on the ground, yelling "fuck" at the top of my lungs. The case flew out and I was back in business.

If there was one day I was supposed to be killed in Vietnam, this was it. Even forgiving the Army for being so fucking stupid loading the first sortie up with shovels to face machine guns, there was the bullet that passed me and hit Bill, the elephant grass that blinded us, the grenade that exploded above us, the M-16 that wouldn't fire.

Is there a God? You bet there is.

He manifest Himself that day in every guy who had come to trust every other guy. No slackers. Not one. Griffin taught us what to do. Mutual respect, trust, and love for each other—something we wouldn't admit to at the time—guided our actions. Training? Sure. Courage? You bet. But most of all we loved life, our own and each other's—this day and throughout our time in Hell together. Great men all: Garland, Zahn, Fisher, Fauvre, Bonds, Cox, Brummett, Almonroder, DeTemple, King, Soyk, Carter, Cooper, Flores, Torres, Bostock.

Chapter 17

Bonehead Bureaucracy

I hope to see my Pilot face to face
When I have crossed the bar.
Alfred, Lord Tennyson, *Crossing the Bar*

Binoculars are not regular issue equipment for a combat infantry squad leader, and I forget why I needed them for this operation, but anyway I did and so signed out a pair from supply.

We were coming to the end of the operation—several days, two weeks, I don't remember—and headed toward a predetermined rendezvous point where, once we secured a landing zone, hueys would swarm down and transport us back to base camp. Before we reached the LZ, however, somewhere in our vicinity a plane went down. While the rest of the company would proceed as planned to get their asses out of there, I was ordered to lead my squad, reinforced with machine gun crew and radio operator, on a search and rescue mission: find the pilot; retrieve the plane's black box; and figure out a way to get back to camp.

Whoever knew that the plane went down and ordered our present mission suggested that the pilot may have ejected. They provided a general area where the plane crashed, and we had become fairly accomplished at reading those sorry aerial photos that substituted for maps in Vietnam. After awhile—again, actual time frames for these episodes don't exist for me anymore—we came upon fragments of the wreck. This caused heart-thumping encouragement because it gave me cause to believe that we might actually be able to rescue the pilot. Frankly, I didn't give a flying shit about looking for, much less finding, a black box in the middle of the jungle that camouflaged a force of unknown size, capable of shooting an airplane out of the air.

Although we had come upon small pockets of metallic debris, we had not yet seen large enough chunks of fuselage to approximate the sight of the crash. Happening upon a narrow river, not readily apparent on the "map," we stopped to devise a strategy, figuring that we shouldn't cross until we made a more thorough search of the side we were on. The sound of gunshots from the other side demanded our immediate attention and determined the course of action.

There was no beach, if rivers have beaches, just jungle with tree tops leaning over the water like a scene from a Tarzan movie. Almost directly across from my position I saw what turned out to be parachute straps suspended, taut, from within the boughs of a tree into the water. My heart sank.

I shed my gear, stripped to the waist, took off my boots, and unsheathed my bayonet. The machine gun crew laid down a base of fire to cover me as I entered what turned out to be deeper water than I expected. When I surfaced near the other bank, the current had washed me about three or four yards below the straps' point of entry. I grabbed branches or vines or something and dragged myself closer to the straps, not letting myself think about what might be suspended from them; I knew, of course, but I couldn't think about it. About him. Not now. No emotion. Get the job done.

I touched the body. Actually, the drift caused it to bump against my legs before I could grasp the straps. It was a couple of feet below the surface. I hacked at one strap until it snapped, wrapped it around my left hand and wrist, then did the same to the other. Adrenaline took over and propelled me and my burden back to the safety of the squad. I remember noticing that the load was surprisingly light and figuring that probably the water and buoyancy or something like that had something to do with the absence of drag.

Someone grabbed my free hand and pulled me out. Someone else grabbed the straps. Physically and emotionally spent, I turned to see the pilot. I had to know at least what he looked like. I never found out. He was decapitated. And from about the waist on his left side and below there was nothing. No hip. No leg. Not even blood. All that remained was a naked, bloated carcass. I retched violently. I probably cried. If I didn't then, I have since. Someone wrapped him in a poncho and we made our way back to camp.

Good ol' base camp. Relative safety, mosquito nets over cots, hot food, cold beer. Rear echelon personnel. Accountability. Paper work. Chicken shit. Supply had to account for the binoculars I left at the river, someone told me. No, I have no fucking idea where the fucking binoculars are, I said. Or words to that effect. Why don't you get the fuck off of your fucking ass and go find the fucking things yourself? Or words to that effect.

They, whoever they were, threatened to dock my next month's pay for the price of the fucking binoculars. Who you gonna charge for the airplane, Asshole?

Chapter 18

Speaking of Virginity

"I pray the gods some respite from the weary task of the long year's watch . . . ."

Aeschylus, *Agamemnon*

Rest and Relaxation, R&R it's called. Commanders since at least the days of Homer have acknowledged the absolute need for warriors to leave the battlefield, if only for a little while, to do whatever soldiers feel they need to do to replenish themselves and then return to the terrible business of war. For the American GI in Vietnam that meant four nights and three days in an exotic Oriental playland. For this GI, that meant Hong Kong.

There I was, a twenty-one year old combat weary stud. A guy can dream, can't he? Indulge me. In the phantasmagoria of my own mind I was a twenty-one year old combat weary stud prepared to party for four nights and three days and never go to sleep. If I was going to die in 1967, I would shuffle off this mortal coil in Hong Kong, not Vietnam, and I would materialize at the pearly gates with beer breath and one huge, dopey, euphoric grin. Here I am, Hong Kong. Amuse me. Take your best shot.

Okay, replied Hong Kong, less than ten minutes after I checked into the Grand Hotel. Prepare to be amused, you twenty-one year old combat weary stud. Mind you, in civilian life I had never been farther west than Philadelphia, and I had never stayed at a hotel before. Yet there I was, checked into my own room in the Kowloon Grand Hotel, a twenty-one-year-old, ready-to-party-till-I-drop, All-American stud. Knock-knock.

I couldn't answer the door right away, because I was in the midst of doing the one thing I longed to do more than anything else, anything. I was sitting in private on a clean toilet caressing the softest roll of toilet paper in the world. I didn't actually have to go, mind you. I was just sitting there savoring my little corner of hygienic heaven. Knock-knock. Ah, crap. Hold on. Right there.

Hello, Hong Kong! A beautiful Chinese girl stood smiling at my door. "Hi, GI," she purred. "You like me?" Stammer, stammer. Holy shit. "Well sure, sure I like you, but I just got here, and, well, I just got here, and, well, uh well, I just got here, and I have to, well sure I like you, I'm sorry will you excuse me, maybe later." Slam. Phew. Holy shit.

Less than five minutes later, the scene repeated itself with a different beautiful Chinese girl standing at my door. Holy shit. Five minutes after that, a third. By the time the inevitable fourth knock-knock sounded, I had composed myself. I planned to open the door and politely tell the beautiful Chinese girl purring in the hall that I already had a date for the evening and needed time to prepare, so thank you very much but please excuse me and please relate my condolences to whomever else might be waiting to befriend this twenty-one-year-old, combat-weary, ready-to-party-until-he-drops, all-American stud. I didn't get the chance to deliver those eloquent lines.

I opened the door only to find a skinny, sleazy, Chinese, twenty-something male standing somewhat bemused before me. Before I could retract my jaw which had dropped to my chest, he asked through a squinty grin, "What are you, queer?" I reached for him half-heartedly and let him hustle away down the hall. "Crazy fucking GI," he grumbled, "crazy."

I wasn't crazy. I don't think I was crazy. Virgins aren't crazy just because they're virgins. Maybe not all twenty-one year old combat weary soldiers fit the stud-in-waiting myth after all. Despite the popular "make love, not war" tee-shirt slogan of the '60s, I knew deep down that getting laid in Hong Kong had nothing to do with making love. Combat veterans know better than anyone else possibly can that war stinks. And I've got to believe that promiscuity ain't so great either.

God, it felt good to perch on that porcelain throne, in private, without gagging on reeking human waste and diesel fuel inside a make-shift three-holer. Maybe I am crazy, after all. Rest and relaxation began with taking a dump.

Chapter 19

Fraternizing at the Chu Lai Sports Bar

The relation between superiors and inferiors is like that between the wind and the grass. The grass must bend when the wind blows across it.

Confucius

And now, as broadcast legend Paul Harvey might say, the rest of the (earlier) story. Maybe a full year after the post track meet at Fort Devens, and after a tough stretch in the jungle, I was sitting drunk on a stool in the make-shift NCO club—a tent—in our base camp at Chu Lai (I had made sergeant).

In comes Captain Michael T. Ruane (he was promoted during the tour and commanded another company at the time) with Lieutenant Tim Sullivan, my former platoon leader. They may have been drunk, too, who knows? Maybe not. Doesn't matter. I thoroughly enjoyed this first and only opportunity to socialize with officers in the combat zone; back in the States that would have been entirely out of the question. Two or three drinks into the conversation—my twentieth or fiftieth of the night—for some reason I remembered the post track meet at Fort Devens.

Yes, they remembered too. "Thanks, Sir," I think I slurred to Captain Ruane. I don't know what you did or said, but I know you had something to do with that hurdles situation, you know, when Lieutenant Whatshisface wanted me to run the quarter mile intermediates. "Yup," he said. "Sure do. We had a lot of money riding on you in that race. If you lost, your ass was grass . . . ."

Chapter 20

News at Six, Film at Eleven

*The press is a sort of wild animal in our midst . . .[acknowledging]
accountability to no one except its owners and publishers.*

Zechariah Chafee, Jr., *The Press under Pressure*

We, the troops, hardly ever knew where we were going when we fell out in front of our tents in base camp. We usually had our packs prepared because we could never anticipate when we were going to be called out. We stacked as many C-ration cans as would fit into a black or olive drab Army-issued sock, and tied the sock to the cross strap on the harness in back. This left room in the pack for toiletries and a change of underwear and socks, and for me a bottle of Tabasco sauce to disguise the taste of the canned crap. For some guys, Bobby Fisher in particular, a full pack also meant writing paper; no matter where we went or for how long, Bobby kept up his correspondence.

On this particular occasion, we fell out with full gear and were actually given specific orders. A platoon from the First Division, "The Big Red One," had been out in the jungle and had lost radio contact. We would chopper to somewhere near their last known location, drop into an as yet undetermined LZ, and find them.

The LZ turned out to be mostly tall grass, maybe knee high. The Hueys had .60-caliber machine guns on either side. Depending on the conditions at the drop site, their gunners would lay down a base of fire to keep the enemy at bay— this is what would happen at a "hot" LZ, one at which the enemy initiated the action. For the VC, this could be a really stupid thing to do, because a sortie of helicopters—usually ten—meant twenty machine guns, ten on each side, spitting out a whole shit-load of fire power.

The VC waited in the wood line until we jumped off the Hueys and the birds flew away. Then, with us in the open and them dug in at fortified positions along the jungle's edge, they opened fire, effectively pinning us down in the elephant grass. The commander called in an air strike: B-52s dropping 500-pound bombs. A second sortie of choppers delivered more good guys and another contingent we hadn't expected. Somehow a news crew got wind of the fact that there was probably going to be action on this mission and they appeared, ready to record history for the news-starved American public.

The bombers made two or three more passes, and at one point drenched the jungle with napalm, a small distance beyond the line which, if we could ever get there, would be our point of entry. We were doing everything right. Lined across in disciplined squads, we advanced one fire team at a time. It was taking a long time to go a short distance; but we weren't suffering casualties at this point, and were in fact getting closer to the jungle.

From out of nowhere, this cameraman runs out in front of us and turns his back to the enemy so he can film us charging automatic gunfire. I didn't think then that he was particularly brave. Just stupid. A "flopper," Sergeant Griffin would have called him. I still think that. More than that, in retrospect I suspect strongly that he was at least professionally ambitious, and most probably greedy. Not idealistic. Actually, the more I think about it, the more I resent his and the news crew's presence.

We had dropped into this maelstrom in full battle gear on a grim and serious mission. (We read later in *Stars and Stripes* that we had fought in a major battle called Operation Attleboro.) Moreover, virtually all of us on the front line were young draftees, who had never voted or drank legally in our home towns, with no burning desire to kill or be killed.

This crazy fuck was a mercenary, trying—hoping, maybe even praying— to capture a poignant portrait of human suffering, maybe mine, that would coincidentally immortalize himself. And what if he happened, oh so fortuitously, to aim his lens right at my neck, the identical spot where Charley was aiming his AK-47, and he zoomed in just as the bullet blew my esophagus into smithereens and my spine shattered between the third and fourth vertebrae and you couldn't tell whether the blood was spurting from the front of my neck or the back or my ears or out of my eye sockets? Would Americans tuned into the evening news really be better off having had the opportunity to watch me die? How would my parents feel if that became their final snapshot of me? I'd like to shove that camera up your cocky civilian ass, you mercenary bastard.

We finally secured the wood line. Charley felt he held us off long enough, I guess, and retreated. On with the mission. Not very deep into what remained of the defoliated jungle, we found them. Dead. All dead. Mangled, hideously distorted, bullet-riddled bodies lay strewn about the tight perimeter. These guys who were just like us, who had never voted or drank legally in their home towns, who had no burning desire to kill or be killed, died. Film footage. Cinema verité. Sergeant Jim Bostock would ask me a day or two later over a cup of C-ration coffee if I had seen the squad leader, a buck sergeant like himself at the time, if I had seen "that buck's" eyeballs dangling down his cheeks like marbles at the end of twin Slinkys. I had. Months later Jim himself died in battle.

We dug a perimeter of foxholes around theirs and set about the gruesome task of carrying the Dead out to the LZ for dustoff. The scene at dusk was surreal. Riflemen genuflecting like those little green toy soldiers you buy 100 to a bag at the Five-and-Ten, pointing their rifles toward no place in particular. Others frantically digging foxholes. The rest hauling away bodies wrapped in ponchos. Even the jungle itself belied its nature. The napalm had stripped away the green and, here and there, left dripping pink globs. It looked like the aftermath of a forest fire. A forest fire without smoke. Everything was dead. The platoon. The fucking trees. And bushes. Dead. All dead.

The gallant news crew decided that they would make it back to wherever the choppers were taking our Dead. I heard one of them say that he didn't think there was going to be any more action, so they had no reason to stay the night. Now, how the fuck could he know that? They'd hitch a ride on the last sortie. How nice to be able to choose where to spend the night in a war zone, while the grunts whose blood and bones and flesh your alchemy reduced to celluloid, while they never had a choice about where they would spend the night. And who would pray to God that the hot shot news guys were right, that there would be no more action that night. Fuck you.

The news guys didn't know squat. Pity they missed the sporadic sniper shots penetrating our perimeter from the sanctuary of black night they owned, or the crack of bullets spinning out of a rifle barrel followed instantly by anguished human screams. Pity they missed the exploding Claymore mines we had set out before nightfall in front of our foxholes and hoped Charley hadn't sneaked up and turned them back toward us before we triggered them. Pity they missed the joy of spending a sleepless night in a shell-shocked sepulcher that stank of rotting flesh and stale blood and sweet gunpowder. Pity they missed the opportunity to freeze-frame the guy who got killed taking a piss in front of his own foxhole. Maybe a Stateside editor would have vetoed that photo anyway. Maybe not. Pity.

I never got to say, "Think I'll catch the last sortie out of here, Mr. Hemingway. How about you?" Yes, I resent that.

Chapter 21

Going Home

*A man travels the world over in search of what he needs
and returns home to find it.*

George Moore, *The Brook Kerith*

I was very short: three weeks or so left to my tour. One of the cadence
songs we sang during training at Fort Devens—how many years ago
was that—rang clearly in my mind: Three more weeks and I'll be
home, / Drinking beer and pissing foam. Legally. Not so fast, GI.

Months before, we had moved up to a small base camp at Chu Lai, I
Corps, right on the coast of the South China Sea. We had actually back-filled a
Marine camp, because they moved farther north, nearer to the DMZ. Less than a
month to go. I can get through this. Piece of cake.

"Company A, fall out."

The first, second, and third platoons saddled up for another one of those
missions of who knows how long. The fourth platoon was the mortar platoon in a
rifle company, and we only tried once early into the tour to take them with us on
patrol. Their equipment—tubes, base plates, shells—proved too cumbersome to
carry through the woods; and unless we were set up in a fairly well-defined

perimeter, giving them the space they needed to operate effectively was impossible. So a company-size exercise consisted of however many men were left in the three rifle platoons.

Most of the territory in and around Chu Lai was considered hostile and had, in fact, been designated "black" areas, or "free fire" zones.[12] Although any Vietnamese we encountered out there could be considered the enemy, our mission turned out to be somewhat nebulous. We were to sweep a broad area and, if the Vietnamese we came upon offered no armed resistance, we were to corral them and call in choppers which then would take them to a relocation camp. They were, after all, presumed VC or at least VC sympathizers.

The operation lasted about two weeks—this one I can remember because, oh, man, I had only three weeks to go. We engaged an occasional sniper or two but got into no major fire fight; and along the way we evicted scores of farming folk from their land. If they were VC, I figured years later, at least they knew what they were fighting for.

On what turned out to be the last day before the last night of my last mission, there we were in box formation again, second squad out front. One freaking week to go! Out ahead, I spotted an adult male, fairly tall for a Vietnamese, trying to hide behind a tree. I don't know whether anyone else saw him yet, but he obviously saw us. Curiously, instead of running directly away from us, he headed from our left to right and just a bit deeper into the woods.

The night before I remember slinging a hammock I had acquired from one of the hootches we had evacuated between two trees behind my foxhole. One week to go. I'm laid out in this spoil of war, puffing a Pall Mall beneath my poncho, daydreaming at night about partying until I dropped in the "real world." Now, I'm leading the squad that's leading the company through hostile territory, and I see this suspected enemy person. Why would he be running, if he wasn't the enemy?

Here's how smart the 1966 Fort Devens 120-yard high hurdles champion and second leg on the 440-yard relay team champion is. I take off after him. Full sprint, out in front of the squad and the entire company, into the jungle. Alone. The good guys properly maintained formation and followed the way they should.

I caught him. I remember thinking during the chase, you stupid fuck, you're going to get killed. But the thrill of the race must have overwhelmed me; and, yes, I know how crazy that sounds. I was too close to him to stop, which is of course exactly what I should have done. I managed to tackle him from behind and smash his face into the ground. Totally overpowered and in no position to offer any more meaningful resistance, he effectively surrendered.

Now fully prepared to be scared to death, I looked around. I hadn't run myself or the company into an ambush, thank God, and the good guys were closing in. Maybe five yards or so ahead of us stood a hootch that blended into the jungle scene like wallpaper. As I started to get off my beaten foe, he squirmed and struggled, trying to get to the door. I wouldn't let him, of course. He ranted frantically on the verge of tearful frustration. Was he yelling at me? Was he warning his buddies? Shut the fuck up, man.

The good guys surrounded the hootch, and I guess they checked for booby traps. Then someone pulled back the curtain that served as a door, while I restrained my prisoner. He went limp. I released him. He was no threat at that point. He rose to his feet and rushed inside. When I got there a few seconds later, I saw him hugging his family: wife, two children, and an elderly lady. Hanging along the full length of one wall was a flag of the Republic of South Vietnam. My suspected enemy and his family huddled in a dingy corner of I Corps weren't the enemy. They were the very people we were fighting for.

Talk about a profile in courage. This guy risked his life running out in front of a heavily armed rifle company that he had been warned was authorized to shoot at will. All he wanted to do was go home, to protect his family as best he could.

I don't really know why I didn't shoot that guy as soon as I spotted him. And the more I think about it, the happier I am that I broke the rules. Chances were very high that, if I hadn't run out in front of the patrol like a flopper, someone else would have shot to kill. And succeeded.

That final episode taught me the lesson I needed to take home with me. For me, mostly, at first, but now for all readers who have come with me this far in my story. Neither the Army nor the war had turned me into a cold-blooded killing machine. At the end of my tour, I valued life infinitely more than its destruction. That man's life—and his wife's, and children's, and mother-in-law's, and countrymen's—was every bit as important, and fragile, as mine. My instinct was to protect life, not to snuff it out on a whim, despite having spent nearly a year training for war and another mired in it.

It took me a long time back in civilian life to understand that insight. Once I accepted the fact that, even though war surely shaped me in some ways, it couldn't corrupt my basic nature. I was then free to believe the same about all other veterans. All we really ever wanted to do was go home.

Chapter 22

My Cousin Dennis

And it's Oh! In my heart, how I wish him safe at home!
Dorothea Jordan, *The Blue Bells of Scotland*

On the last morning of my last mission we broke camp and headed toward an LZ that the 12th Armored Cavalry Division had secured for us. Actually, I didn't know who had set up the perimeter for our evacuation, but it always felt good to see a bunch of tanks with their guns lowered to point blank range aiming menacingly into the jungle. It turns out that my cousin Dennis with whom I had been corresponding was a tank driver in that outfit. We, the 196th, had been near elements of the 12th Cav before, and I always asked if Dennis' squadron was in the area. It never was.

In order to get to the LZ, we had to cross a river which formed a great natural defensive position on one side—the side, it turns out, at which we would enter the perimeter. Having sacrificed a couple of shirt buttons during the tussle the day before, I emerged from the water looking like a skinny, sopping GI Joe plucked out of a washing machine. One or two inquiries to the first tankers we met yielded the almost unbelievable good fortune that, yes, Spec-4 Russell was right over there, a few tanks away.

He could hardly have expected to see me any more than I expected to see him. I resisted the urge to run, but nevertheless hustled myself from tank to tank inside the perimeter. There he was. Unbelievable. In the early morning light, I saw Dennis Russell sitting on a blanket, beneath a makeshift shelter he had rigged off the side of his tank with his poncho, playing poker with his tank commander. "Hey, Paul," he shouted before I realized he had even seen me. (You've got to know how seriously the Russell men take their cards to understand the compliment he was paying me.) Hand shakes, hugs, introductions, more hand shakes, more hugs. I don't remember either Dennis or Sergeant Whoever even picking up the pot. What a phenomenal scene.

"So, Paul, you want a beer?"

"Are you kidding? Sure."

"What kind?"

These guys had four cases of amber nectar stashed somewhere on that mobile, rumbling, grumbling arsenal. On ice! Good God Almighty, it doesn't get any better than this. We had a beer together, and I don't remember one blessed thing we talked about. But I'll never forget Dennis' smiling face that day, my last day in the boonies of Vietnam. Before I returned home, home came to me somewhere in the middle of I Corps in the northeast quadrant of South Vietnam. The presence of the tanks insured my physical safety; Dennis being there put my heart at ease. Good God Almighty, it doesn't get any better than this.

Not too long after that, family and friends and it seemed like all of Harrison threw me a party at my brother-in-law's tavern. God, it was great to be home. Uncle Eddie—my mother's brother, Dennis' father—asked just a bit coyly, "Did you ever run into Dennis over there?"

"Well, yes. Yes I did," I teased.

"How is he? Where was we? How'd you come to see him? What was he doing? How does he look?" He bombarded me with questions, and I knew, at least this once in my life, I held the upper hand on a family elder. I responded unemotionally with all the understatement I could muster.

"All I can tell you is this, Uncle Eddie. When I saw Dennis, he was drinking beer and playing poker."

"That's my boy!" he screamed with great delight.

Hand shakes. Hugs. More hugs. "Come over here, everybody. Wait 'till you hear this. Go ahead, Paul, tell them. Tell them everything."

It's hard to capture, much less describe, the feelings I experienced that night in Paul's Pub. I had returned to all these people I loved and who loved me. And from then on I never felt funny about using that word. They didn't ask me questions or want me to talk about the war or the jungle or anything like that. They were just genuinely glad to see me.

I was home. And now I wanted Dennis to be home. Mixed in with the warm serenity I felt at my own happy circumstance was the chilling knowledge that Dennis was still there. In an instant, my psyche was flooded with conflicting, confusing emotions. All at once I knew what it was like to leave home (bold), to travel to war (anxious), to fight (afraid, empty, animalistic, brave, fulfilled, human), to return (spent) in need of physical, emotional, and spiritual rejuvenation, and finally to care deeply for someone else's safe return (helpless). While family and friends had not experienced my war, I now shared theirs.

Part IV

Calm After the Storm

1967–85

Chapter 23

Back Home and Back to College

1967–70

Follow your bliss.

Joseph Campbell, *The Power of Myth*

On July 15, 1967, I mustered out of the Army in Oakland, California. Jersey natives Willie Bonds, Bobbie Fisher, Bob Fauvre and I— together since the very beginning: civilians stepping forward to take the oath of service at the induction center in Newark, yard birds polishing the turd that was Fort Dix—blew a big chunk of our severance pay on First Class tickets on a non-stop red-eye to John F. Kennedy International Airport in New York. From there, we parted company, and I took a taxi to my father's place of business on Waverly Place in Greenwich Village. I arrived before he did. The family knew I was in the country, but not that I was literally on my way home, so for Dad this was just another work day.

Standing in my newly issued summer greens outside his shop sucking down whatever I was smoking that day—a habit I had acquired from the hundreds of C-ration packages I consumed overseas—I could see the back of his hatted head emerging from the subway stairwell a little way down the block.

Having never thought about what this moment would be like, I froze momentarily. Then, as he reached the sidewalk and turned toward the shop, I approached slowly enough for him to focus and see me. Four or five of his coworkers, who had figured out who I was and had assembled in anticipation of the reunion, applauded and cheered the hug. He introduced me to them with an expression in his eyes I had never seen: part pride, I'm sure, but mostly a serene joy that I didn't fully recognize or understand then but appreciate now that I have children of my own. Father and son, to be sure, but our man-boy relationship had forever changed.

We crossed the street to a coffee shop and shared two things we never shared before, coffee and cigarettes. I felt awkward sitting face-to-face, alone in a crowded, noisy breakfast joint, with this man for whom small talk did not exist. To break the early silence I pointed to the decorations on my chest.

"Know what that is?" I asked, pointing to the ribbon version of the Bronze Star.

"Yes."

"Want to know why I got it?"

"No."

Dad gave me a subway token and directions home. (I needed neither, but he needed to give them to me.) His immediate call to Mom instigated a hasty gathering of available family members to greet me at 305 Ann Street in an hour or so. She had painted Revolutionary War sentries on a pair of wooden ironing boards, attached them to the porch pillars, and joined them with a "Welcome Home" banner across the lintel. God, what a feeling when I got there! The hugs lingered and tears flowed freely. I really was home.

Friends and relations visited throughout the day, mostly after the work day. Sometime that evening, while we talked around the dining room table, someone asked, "How many gooks did you kill?" In a heartbeat my father interjected emphatically, "Don't ever ask him that again." (I needed him to say that.)

A few nights later, Mom asked that I go with her to the adult art class she taught at the public library. As her students saw us enter the room, without a word they put their brushes down and greeted us with gentle applause and warm smiles—not unlike the one my father had displayed on the sidewalk in New York. Embarrassed, I accepted their lingering handshakes and thanked each personally. One after the other said in so many words, "We've been praying for you for a year." God, what a feeling! My presence among them, attached umbilically hand in hand with my mother, validated their faith in the power of prayer.

Within two weeks or so I returned to the furniture moving business. My friends all had real jobs; those who had stayed in college graduated or had at most a year to go; in a year or two most of them would be married. Without dwelling on it at the time, I began to realize that, while my life had taken such a dramatic detour over the past two years, my friends' lives—what I considered normal lives—progressed pretty much on schedule. Some avoided the draft somehow and got jobs after high school and married. Most went to college, developed relationships, graduated, landed career path jobs, and married. I had no job, no degree, no girl friend, no direction. I felt alienated, not so much because I had been away in Vietnam, but simply because I had been away. Their lives and mine were no longer in synch.

I sought guidance from two men I admired and whose opinions I respected: my brother Charlie and my brother-in-law Paul Heaney. I told them that I felt I should return to college, even though I still wasn't exactly sure what I wanted to study. Education kept creeping into the conversation, maybe physical education. With only about a month before the opening of the fall semester, however, prospects for actually getting into a college right away were dim. Well, it turned out that Paul's brother Jimmy knew the Director of Admissions at Upsala College in East Orange. He would tell him about me and my situation. He did, and I matriculated as a liberal arts major that September. In less than two months I went from jungle fatigues to button-down shirts, from bunker to classroom. Night patrols hunting for an elusive enemy gave way to evening trips to the library where I did my homework in literature, psychology, public speaking, and philosophy and, also, kept on the lookout for members of the opposite sex, a species I found almost as elusive as the Viet Cong. God, it felt good to be normal again, even if I trailed my friends by a couple of years and didn't exactly fit in with my classmates.

I left Upsala, a private school with steep tuition, after one semester strictly for financial reasons. This may have been another in my continuous line of bone head decisions.

Except for that one year of night classes at Jersey City State, ever since sixth grade, school and sports went together for me. I tried to join the Upsala football team. John Hooper, the head coach and athletic director, advised me to concentrate on getting back into the habit of studying. Technically, I was a transfer student and had to sit out a year of intercollegiate competition anyway. I agreed reluctantly, but kept a locker and began track workouts every day on my own. It turned out that Coach Hooper also coached the track team and his assistant, Harold Jardine, retired long-time coach at Kearny High School, made himself available regularly at the track for out-of-season runners. Mr. Jardine remembered me from my high school days, and we quickly developed a great rapport. I dug a few hurdles out of storage as soon as I could, and he watched me rekindle the love affair and encouraged me every day.

During that semester, things went fairly well. I bought a Volkswagen Beetle for $1,867, turned my monthly GI Bill checks over to my mother for management purposes (she took care of car and tuition payments for me and we split whatever was left), and earned spending money tending bar at my brother-in-law's tavern, Paul's Pub, in Harrison. Coincident with my application to Upsala I had also applied to Montclair State College, which like Jersey City State, was also predominantly a teachers college. Toward the end of the semester I received notification that they were considering me for acceptance. The arithmetic was simple: two GI Bill installments would pay for an entire year at Montclair.

I approached Mr. Hooper to tell him that I would like to stay at Upsala, but basically I was there to say goodbye. He asked me to come back in a couple of days, which I did. At that time, he gave me a proposition I probably should not have refused. He told me that Upsala was prepared to offer me a full scholarship, minus my GI Bill benefits. In other words, in return for turning over my monthly government checks to the college, I would attend Upsala at no additional cost. Instead, I entered Montclair State in January, the spring semester of 1968, and, after two months, had more than $300 in my pocket each month to split with Mom. Because of NCAA regulations, this most recent transfer meant that I couldn't compete intercollegiately until spring semester 1969.

As luck would have it, Mr. Jardine had accepted an assistant coaching position at Montclair. The head track coach, Dr. George Horn, turned out to be an incredible human being whose nephew had been captured by the North Vietnamese. The coaches and I hit it off marvelously and, despite my ineligibility to compete right away for the college, they arranged to enter me "unattached" in open meets, including all those in Madison Square Garden in 1969.

In my first outing, I toed the line at an indoor pre-season development meet at the 168th Street Armory in New York—first time in competition since the Fort Devens Post Championship in 1966 and first time against serious competition since the Outdoor Metropolitan Championships on Randall's Island in 1964. Because of my extended hiatus, I wasn't seeded in the 60-yard highs. Nevertheless, I placed well in the first round and again in the semi-finals. In the finals I placed second or third. Very few people there knew me then, especially running unattached in a plain grey tee shirt. But throughout the meet I had seen my former coach from Manhattan standing, stop watch in hand, near the finish line. Instead of returning right away to the starting area to retrieve my sweats after the final, I jogged over to him and said, "Mr. McHugh, remember me?" "Yes, Paul," he replied. "I'm running again." I honestly don't think he wished me any ill will when I left Manhattan College, but I felt I had to bring closure to that relationship, and rid myself of the "you'll never run again" bogey.

The next year I proudly wore the Montclair State red and white as I took my mark in a preliminary heat of the Millrose Games against then reigning Olympic Champion, Willie Davenport. In an eye blink over seven seconds he broke the tape with me stepping off the last hurdle, less than five yards behind. That's about a giant-step-and-a-half. The three other timber toppers in the heat finished ahead of me, too. That didn't matter at all. I had come a long, long way from Vietnam. God I loved running the high hurdles!

In the spring of '69 Montclair ran against Upsala, then in the fall we played them in football. Before and after each event, I exchanged cordial greetings with Coach Hooper. What a gentleman.

Ho Hum

Ho Chi Minh died of a heart attack on September 3, 1969.

Life Continues, So Does the War

Most students at Montclair State, including me, commuted. This didn't impress me at the time as having any significance until I placed it within the context of activities occurring on other campuses across the country (assuming the media were reporting them accurately). Anti-war demonstrations, allegedly student-led, appeared regularly on newscasts: sit-ins, marches, draft card burnings, that sort of thing. None of that at Montclair. That pleased me because I definitely wanted to avoid confrontations with what I considered to be mostly draft avoiders (males) and vociferous, often obnoxious, coeds who exploited the luxury of trying to sound brave and tough in a sheltered environment within which they had little chance of being held accountable for their actions. No matter how outrageous their behavior, the Constitution protected protesting students, male and female. Suddenly, the unbelievable happened at Kent State.

On May 4, 1970, the Vietnam War hit home for Americans. And it hit hard. President Richard Nixon's recent order to conduct air strikes over Cambodia caused increased anti-war activity on college campuses because of the escalation this action implied. At Kent State University (Ohio), students went so far as to try to burn the ROTC building. Governor James Rhodes sent in the National Guard. In the end, four civilians lay dead, nine others fell wounded by Guardsmen firing M-1 rifles.

Combat veterans know that every bellicose action in war bears consequences. They know, for example, that rifle shots and artillery rounds don't always hit intended targets. Often they miss, and sometimes unintended victims—innocent people—suffer. Innocence fell at Kent State and the nation suffered. The line between good guys and bad guys disappeared.

To avert rampant chaos, college administrators around the country called for moratoriums at their schools, a suspension of regular classes so that academic communities could discuss the emotional, divisive issues of the day such as the tragic loss of life at Kent State, the anti-war movement, the war itself, freedom of speech, the right to assemble, and so on. What a great idea.

This was my final semester, student teaching was over, I was about to graduate. I had chosen Government and Politics in the Far East as my last undergraduate elective during that final mini-term, specifically because of its timely relevance for me, for everyone. I hoped to gain some academic perspective of the history and culture of those people I had encountered under most difficult circumstances.

When Montclair State invoked the moratorium, the lesson I learned befuddled me. Theoretically, students would follow regular class schedules. No attendance would be taken. Students could meet with teachers and with each other, assemble as usual, or break off into self-defined mini-groups. I arrived early at the classroom, eager to participate, anxious to hear what the instructor had to say. He was a young African teaching at an American public college about Asian political structures to soon-to-be high school teachers. Dynamite. What a unique combination. I waited and waited. Nobody showed, not even the teacher.

The student body—remember, mostly commuters—seized the dispensation, handed to them on the platter of canceled classes, and headed en masse for the Jersey Shore for a day at the beach. I knew then that so many rag-tag, pseudo-intellectual, sex, drug, and rock 'n roll loving pacifists were just plain full of shit. They didn't care about conscripted Americans, the Vietnamese people (North or South), Cambodians, or fellow students in Ohio, California, Alabama, or anywhere else. They cared only about themselves, most of them. Charter members of the Me Generation, they grew up taking and taking; never giving, never serving. They took everything their hard working, self-sacrificing parents offered them including, for many, a college education. And they let suckers like me do their fighting. When asked collectively to pause, to explore intellectually the burning issues of the day, these would-be future leaders went AWOL to the beach. There were no consequences to this action. No one would have to stand before an authority figure and listen to anything resembling "Your ass is grass."

I learned much about myself and others in Vietnam, and then I learned much I didn't want to believe about my generation in general in college. In Vietnam,

I trusted my buddies with whom I shared hardship, uncertainty, and, ultimately, genuine collegiality. Back home, I came to doubt the motives of transient denizens of ivy-covered institutions, students and faculty alike, whose life experiences did not correspond to my own.

Vietnam veterans are different. Unlike those who hid behind, or in front of, desks and camouflaged themselves as intellectuals during the war, we passed life's greatest tests. During the '60s and '70s, students and instructors held hands during Psychology 101 trust walks. We pressed our hands against gaping wounds, so our comrades wouldn't bleed to death. They triumphantly conducted hostile, well publicized overthrows of administrative offices. We lay at ambush sites, monsoon-drenched and miserable, praying that an involuntary cough or sneeze would not compromise our position. They ambled through life in those days with impunity, while any step we took could be our last. They prepared themselves for the good life. We just wanted to live.

Government and Politics in the Far East never met again that semester. Final grade: "P" for Pass.

Chapter 24

Teaching, a Learning Experience
1970–81

Nothing in education is so astonishing as the amount of ignorance it accumulates in the form of inert facts.
Henry Brooks Adams, *The Education of Henry Adams*

For the remainder of the Vietnam War, I taught and coached, for two years in a private school and then (until 1981) in a public high school. Somewhere during that time I lost the chip I carried on my shoulder about everyone my age who, in whatever way, protested the war. For the most part, if we talked about it at all, fellow teachers expressed respect for my service. Senior colleagues who had lived through the Second World War experience were the most sympathetic. Those a bit younger knew something of the sacrifices made during the Korean War. Although some fellow teachers (males) had served in the military, most fell into the age group that rendered them too young for Korea and too old for Vietnam. Even though they were not called to combat, thank God, they served our country with honor, dignity, and patriotism. The youngest teachers, those about my own age, however, had no clue about any of this. An anachronistic anecdote will explain.

When the movie *Deer Hunter* came out in 1978, a young female teacher with a masters degree in history asked me if I had ever played Russian Roulette during my tour in Vietnam. (A dramatic scene in the movie had American Prisoners of War facing off with loaded pistols pressed against their temples and firing unemotionally for the amusement of their sadistic guards.) She asked this, I'm sure, without ulterior motive. But how stupid can a smart person be? Using her simply as a model, not as a case study, this typifies the problem with book learning without experience. She taught history with no sense of context. Over the years, various acquaintances have said to me after seeing a movie about Vietnam words to this effect: "Now I know what it was like for you guys."

Excuse me. No, you don't. No matter how red the fake blood on screen, no matter how loud the sound effects, no matter how many times actors scream the "F" word, no matter how sympathetic the hero, no, you don't. You don't know what it is like to be shot at, to lie in a trench during a mortar attack, to watch the guy next to you die and wonder why the bullet missed you. You don't know what it is like to fire a weapon at a human being, not a shooting range bulls eye, to throw a hand grenade and hope it inflicts maximum damage. Thank God you don't know these things. But don't kid yourself into thinking you know what combat is like because you saw a movie.

Chapter 25

The Wall
1985

My life with girls has ended, though till lately I was up to it and
soldiered on not ingloriously; now on this wall will hang
my weapons and my lyre, discharged from the war.

Horace, *Ars Poetica*

When the '80s rolled around, I had about as much interest in visiting The Wall as I had in going to see war movies. Little, closer to none. I had wrestled with my demons, and although I couldn't claim outright victory, I was willing to settle for a draw. I wanted to believe that my return to normalcy was complete and so did not cherish the thought of standing before a monument that might rekindle dark memories.

I succeeded in avoiding The Wall for several years after it was built.

Out of the blue—way out of the blue—I received a long distance call from Lowell Garland. Although he had a heck of a time tracking me down, there he was, sitting in Indiana, taking the time to tell me that the 196th was having a reunion in Washington. They—we—were going to lay a wreath at The Wall. We talked for I'm not sure how long. I remember having incredibly mixed emotions. His call thrilled me and scared me at the same time. I think I was terse with him though I didn't mean to be. As it turned out, I was going to Egypt on a business trip during the reunion and wouldn't be able to make it.

Several years later, Eddie Zahn got hold of me from Upper Michigan and convinced me that I had to make it to the next reunion in Boston with a side visit to Fort Devens thrown in for old times sake. In Boston, Lowell and I sat on a curb in the parking lot outside the Holiday Inn, drinking beer and talking deep into the early morning. We caught up on everything, family and work, how we had gotten on with our lives, that kind of thing. Even after all those years and all those beers that night, I remember him bringing up the phone conversation.

"You weren't ready," he said matter of factly. He knew. Sure I had this airtight excuse, being out of the country and all, but that didn't matter. I was infinitely more prepared to climb up to Cheops' burial chamber inside the great pyramid at Giza than I was to go on an archaeological dig into my own psyche. I had spent too much energy since July 1967 sealing my emotions behind a wall. The bricks crumbled that night.

I finally had someone to talk with about what had been swirling around in my screwed up head for so long. How could I tell anyone else about the guilt I felt at leaving Vietnam? It sounded, even to me, so stupid, so fake, almost self-serving. Nevertheless, that is how I truly felt, and I didn't think anyone would believe me, or care. The road to discovery began that night in the motel parking lot. I know now that lots of people care—the guys I served with, all guys who served, friends of both genders and all ages, and family. What I have found is that people don't care much about the particulars—helicopters, machine guns, napalm, fox holes, and all that—they care about the person. They care about me.

I have tried to describe this coming out feeling to myself. This is the best I can do.

Close your eyes and imagine your mind as a jungle—intricate, complex, beautiful, awesome, life threatening. And the rain, the monsoon rain. Can you see it? Smell it. Hear it. Feel it. It teems and teems. A crack of thunder—or was that artillery—then a bolt of lightning. Another and another. You look for shelter but find none. Why do you shiver? Is it the chill of the rain on your parched skin? Or are you scared? It never stops. Never.

And then it stops. The endless storm ends. Forever. The warmth you feel comes from inside your own body. You swallowed the sun. If you don't write poetry, you at least think poetically. If you don't paint landscapes, you at least see them with a new eye. And even if you can't hold a single note, your heart sings. The jungle, the storm, the war can hurt you no more. It is safe to come out.

I arrived at Washington, D.C. the day before I was to give a speech on training to an international audience. It was a beautiful day in the middle of the week in the early spring. Alone, I walked the city, skirting the periphery of the mall. All right, damn it! Time to go to The Wall. Lowell, I'm ready.

I did not expect it to be so magnificent in such a subdued way. I stopped at a directory. Bostock. Cooper. Torres. I read the places where they died. I never heard of them. Our maps didn't have names of places, just coordinates. The Wall brought back memories, mostly good ones. Jim Bostock defying Sergeant Griffin with his too tightly tailored shirts. Dave Cooper smiling through buck teeth and slinging his M-60 machine gun around like a toy. Angelo Torres sitting on the edge of his cot writing to the most beautiful girl in the world back in Chicago.

I stood alone—glad to be alone—facing The Wall, saying a prayer or two, thinking good thoughts. God, I was glad to be there.

An all-American family of four stopped a few feet from me. The youngest sat astride his father's shoulders, his brother held his mother's hand. She wanted to stop. "Come on," the father said with a huff. "I want to see the Lincoln Memorial." "In a minute," she said gruffly. "I think I knew one of these guys."

"Daddy, what is this," the youngest asked in an "are we there yet" kind of tone. "It's just a big rock with the names of a whole bunch of guys who died for nothing," he replied in a "beat it, kid, you bother me" kind of tone. Another time, another place, this jerk gets decked.

The jungle tries to creep back into my mind, a storm brews, the war sits in ambush. No. Don't let it. That can't be. I've come too far. Damn it, I made it to The Wall. I wanted to slam the Ugly American's face into the ground. I wanted to scream at his wife, "He had a name. What was his name? I'll help you find his name." I wanted to tell the kids that their father was a jerk. Most of all I wanted to be alone again, so that nobody would see the warm tears welling in my eyes.

In "Mending Wall," Robert Frost wrote:

Before I built a wall I'd ask to know
What I was walling in or walling out,
And to whom I was like to give offense.

The compassionate company of Willie, Eddie, Paul, and Lowell in Boston tore down my personal wall, the one that locked me in and everyone else out. The wall before me now embraced me. It animated the names etched into its face. And at the same time it stood as a fence that separated me from some people who would never understand, never care. No good could come from a confrontation with ignorance. The storm blew over.

Epilogue

*With malice toward none; with charity for all; with firmness in the right, as
God gives us to see the right, let us strive on to finish the work we are in: to
bind up the nation's wounds; to care for him who shall have borne the battle,
and for his widow and his orphan, to do all which may achieve and cherish a
just and lasting peace among ourselves, and with all nations.*

Abraham Lincoln, *Second Inaugural Address*

At a flea market sometime in 1990, for twenty-five cents I picked up a paperback that caught my eye and in large measure became the prod to my writing this book. The cover of *Ho Chi Minh on Revolution: Selected Writings, 1920–66* proclaims: "Written in prison, exile, and battle, this is the political bible followed by half the world." Inside the front cover this note about the editor appears: "Bernard B. Fall, who edited this volume and provided a notable introductory profile of Ho Chi Minh, was one of the world's foremost authorities on Vietnam. He was killed in South Vietnam by a Viet Cong mine in 1967."

The scholarly thoroughness of the introduction and the flow of the 349 yellowed pages that follow bear witness to the fact that Bernard Fall was not a firefight chasing journalist like the ones I encountered during Operation Attleboro. His work enthralled me, and I got angrier and angrier reading those words of Ho that spanned 46 years. What angered me most was that, although this

$1.25 Signet paperback was published by The New American Library in 1968, I couldn't imagine any American policy maker as having read it or, if he or she had, that it was not taken seriously.

Although I hate Ho's Communism, I can't help but admire his total personal commitment to it. This wasn't Lenin or Stalin or even Mao who lived lives quite different than the one they preached for the masses. This self-professed, life-long revolutionary appears to have been more patriotic than despotic. Fall cites a 1966 television interview with "[o]ne of North Vietnam's severest scholarly critics, Professor P. J. Honey, a lecturer at the University of London ... '[O]ne of the things which has impressed Honey enormously about Ho Chi Minh is how much he learned from Gandhi.'" Fall comments that there "are very few Communist leaders in the world who can evoke such a comparison and even fewer to whom it would actually be applicable." While acknowledging the possibility that Ho's "Gandhi-like deportment" might be just an act, he says, "[I]n fact, Ho Chi Minh ... no doubt play-acts part of the time, and as chief executive of his part of the country he is a captive of his mythology. But it is also true that he *means* to be exactly what he is" (*Ho*, x) [emphasis in the original].

I appreciate Ho Chi Minh's patriotism. Likewise, I appreciate and do not question the patriotism of America's leaders, military and civilian, during the Vietnam War; but I do wonder about their motivations. Eisenhower's Domino Theory proved false. McNamara moved on to a prestigious post with the World Bank. Johnson chose not to run for a second term as president.

The aging, confessional—probably penitent—McNamara writes: "Readers must wonder by now—if they have not been mystified long before—how presumably intelligent, hardworking, and experienced officials—both civilian and military—failed to address systematically and thoroughly questions whose answers so deeply affected the lives of our citizens and the welfare of our nation" (*IR*, 277). To which I respond: Those are your presumptions, not mine, Mr. McNamara. You and your coterie of elitist, intellectual Ivy League snobs presumed yourselves superior when you read and believed your press clippings and compared SAT scores while sipping dry martinis in good ol' boys' clubs that the rest of us could never presume to gain entry to. Further, an intelligent guy like yourself should know that the disease called workaholism dupes its victims into thinking they are producing something when in fact all they are producing is more work for themselves in order to impress others with all the work they are doing and thereby perpetuate their own self-created myths of being hard-working production machines. All your hard work generated reports and white papers and sleeping pill nights and more reports but did not produce a simple mission statement, did not produce a clear military or political strategy, and did not present American soldiers the opportunity to win the war in Vietnam. And as I recall, Mr.

McNamara, you had no combat experience. No, don't kid yourself. We're not mystified. We're bitter. We were betrayed.

Citing the cliché that "[p]eople are human; they are fallible," McNamara concedes "with painful candor and a heavy heart that the adage applies to [himself] and to [his] generation of American leadership regarding Vietnam." He says, "Although we sought to do the right thing—and believed we were doing the right thing ... hindsight proves us wrong" (*IR*, 333). Dead wrong. Sixty thousand American Dead wrong.

To his credit, McNamara added non-flattering points of view to the appendix of the 1996 Vintage Books paperback edition of his memoir. To wit: "Perhaps the only value of *In Retrospect* is to remind us never to forget that these were men who in the full hubristic glow of their power would not listen to logical warning or ethical appeal."[13]

Hubris. Power. Ethics. Aren't these concepts written, discussed, argued about at least as far back in Western history and literature as Homer? If the best and brightest don't learn how to apply these lessons while attending our finest institutions of higher learning, can there be any hope for the rest of us mere mortals?

Yes. There is hope if we exercise our democratic freedoms and responsibilities, if we refuse to allow unethical, egotistical people to gain or retain positions of power. Plato tells us that the best persons to govern are those with happy, productive lives outside the political arena. Professional intellectuals and career politicians require constant reminding that citizen soldiers fight and die in our wars, and ultimately it is they who, when properly supplied, supported, and motivated, win them.

Intellectuals and politicians must never be allowed to refer to men and women in uniform as anything less than human. United States soldiers are not assets; they are people. Our nation's military missions must never again be likened to business plans; they are crusades fought in the name of ideals—freedom, democracy, human rights—not commercial ventures. The vocabulary of "acceptable costs" and "acceptable risks"—convenient euphemisms for stock market investors—must never be associated with human life.

Fall credits Ho's "deceptive simplicity," a Gandhi-like characteristic, for his undeniable popularity among his people. "Most bureaucracies are unwilling to admit mistakes," Fall argues, a point which becomes amply clear to anyone who looks at the Western record in Vietnam over the past twenty years (i.e., 1946–66). Yet, on August 18, 1956, three months before the farmers of his own native province rose in rebellion over the botched land reform which Hanoi had thoughtlessly rammed through, "Ho Chi Minh went on the radio to admit that 'the leadership of the Party Central Committee and of the Government is sometimes lacking in concreteness, and control and encouragement is disregarded. All this has caused us to commit errors and meet with shortcomings in carrying out land reform.'

"The same candor made him state ten years later, on July 17, 1966, that the United States would eventually destroy most of North Vietnam's major cities—a prospect which could hardly have heartened his fellow citizens, but which, under the circumstances, he felt they must face up to. In the same speech, he also promised his people the possibility of war for perhaps another five, ten, or twenty years" (*Ho*, xi).

Ho didn't hide from his people what he believed to be the truth. And they didn't run from it. The war dragged on for another nine years until, on April 30, 1975, the Republic of Vietnam (the South) surrendered unconditionally to the Provisional Revolutionary government of the North.

I do not believe our leaders ever told us what they believed to be the whole truth about Vietnam. Maybe that was because they could never agree on what the truth was. Maybe the truth is, they never really had a clue.

The Government—hence, whomever made up the government—abused its power: it instituted a draft system with too many loopholes; it let those Vietnam veterans who survived struggle alone with their handicaps; and it ignored their sacrifices.

We, the People, must never let that happen again.

Endnotes

1. Bernard B. Fall, ed. *Ho Chi Minh on Revolution: Selected Writings, 1920–66.* New York: Signet Books, 1968, pp. 141–43. In a footnote to this reprinted Declaration of Independence of the Democratic Republic of Vietnam, Fall writes that Ho's "borrowing from the United States Declaration of Independence was open and intended." Subsequent quotations from Bernard Fall's book cited in the text and noted are abbreviated: *Ho.*

2. Death counts, one finds, vary depending on the source (e.g., American or Japanese records). By any reckoning, a great number of non-combatant Japanese died.

3. Tojo Hidecki was Japan's Prime Minister and Minister of War during World War II and approved the attack on Pearl Harbor.

4. "Images '97." *Time*, 22 December 1997: 50. In this photo essay, *Time* cited a World Food Program report that claimed "nearly 2.5 million people in [North Korea] are at risk of starvation."

5. Sun-Tzu. *The Art of Warfare*. Roger Ames, ed. and trans. New York: Ballentine Books, 1993.

6. "Not in my back yard" originated somewhere in the 1980s and usually refers to needed but undesirable facilities such as garbage dumps, incinerators, and nuclear power plants. People generally agree that we need to dispose of waste and search for alternative power sources, but usually, for environmental reasons, they don't welcome the presence of these facilities in their own municipalities.

7. The United States backed an invasion of Cuba by about 1,500 CIA-trained Cuban exiles at the Bay of Pigs. Their goal was to topple the Castro government. The mission failed miserably.

8. McNamara, Robert S. *In Retrospect: The Tragedy and Lessons of Vietnam*. New York: Vintage Books, 1996. Subsequent quotations from Robert McNamara's book cited in the text and noted are abbreviated: *IR*.

9. "In April 1954, President Eisenhower made his famous prediction that if Indochina fell, the rest of Southeast Asia would 'go over very quickly' like a 'row of dominoes'" (*IR*, 31).

10. Article 15 of the Uniform Code of Military Justice allows a commander to mete out punishment with some discretion for relatively minor offenses. Going beyond the limits of a 50-mile pass, for example, was sufficient grounds for an Article 15.

11. I never understood why anyone engaged in this activity would be smiling about it.

12. Before we were sent into black areas, planes dropped propaganda fliers and pamphlets, and also told inhabitants—friends and enemies alike—we were coming.

13. In the Appendix to the Vintage Edition, Editorials/Letters, McNamara included the editorial, "Mr. McNamara's War" from *The New York Times* 12 April 1995 (*IR*, 354).

ARMY MUSEUMS

West of the Mississippi
by Fred L. Bell, SFC Retired

ISBN: 1-55571-395-5
Paperback: 17.95

A guide book for travelers to the army museums of the west, as well as a source of information about the history of the site where the museum is located. Contains detailed information about the contents of the museum and interesting information about famous soldiers stationed at the location or specific events associated with the facility. These twenty-three museums are in forts and military reservations which represent the colorful heritage in the settling of the American West.

BYRON'S WAR

I Never Will Be Young Again...
by Byron Lane

ISBN: 1-55571-402-1
Hardcover: 21.95

Based on letters that were mailed home and a personal journal written more than fifty years ago during World War II, Byron's War brings the war life through the eyes of a very young air crew officer. It depicts how the life of this young American changed through cadet training, the experiences as a crew member flying across the North Atlantic under wartime hazards to the awesome responsibility assigned to a nineteen year-old when leading hundreds of men and aircraft where success or failure could seriously impact the outcome of the war.

K-9 SOLDIERS

Vietnam and After
by Paul B. Morgan

ISBN: 1-55571-495-1
Paperback: 13.95

A retired US Army officer, former Green Beret, Customs K-9 and Security Specialist, Paul B. Morgan has written *K-9 Soldiers*. In his book, Morgan relates twenty-four brave stories from his lifetime of working with man's best friend in combat and on the streets. They are the stories of dogs and their handlers who work behind the scenes when a disaster strikes, a child is lost or some bad guy tries to outrun the cops.

AFTER THE STORM

A Vietnam Veteran's Reflection
by Paul Drew

ISBN: 1-55571-500-1
Paperback: 14.95

Even after twenty-five years, the scars of the Vietnam War are still felt by those who were involved. *After the Storm: A Vietnam Veteran's Reflection* is more than a war story. Although it contains episodes of combat, it does not dwell on them. It concerns itself more on the mood of the nation during the war years, and covers the author's intellectual and psychological evolution as he questions the political and military decisions that resulted in nearly 60,000 American deaths.

GREEN HELL

The Battle for Guadalcanal
by William J. Owens

ISBN: 1-55571-498-6
Paperback: 18.95

This is the story of thousands of Melanesian, Australian, New Zealand, Japanese, and American men who fought for a poor insignificant island is a faraway corner of the South Pacific Ocean. For the men who participated, the real battle was of man against jungle. This is the account of land, sea and air units covering the entire six-month battle. Stories of ordinary privates and seamen, admirals and generals who survive to claim the victory that was the turning point of the Pacific War.

OH, WHAT A LOVELY WAR

A Soldier's Memoir
by Stanley Swift

ISBN: 1-55571-502-8
Paperback: 14.95

This book tells you what history books do not. It is war with a human face. It is the unforgettable memoir of British soldier Gunner Stanley Swift through five years of war. Intensely personal and moving, it documents the innermost thoughts and feelings of a young man as he moves from civilian to battle-hardened warrior under the duress of fire.

THROUGH MY EYES

91st Infantry Division, Italian Campaign 1942-1945   ISBN: 1-55571-497-8
by Leon Weckstein
Paperback: 14.95

Through My Eyes is the true account of an Average Joe's infantry days before, during and shortly after the furiously fought battle for Italy. The author's front row seat allows him to report the shocking account of casualties and the rest-time shenanigans during the six weeks of the occupation of the city of Trieste. He also recounts in detail his personal roll in saving the historic Leaning Tower of Pisa.

Order Directly From Hellgate Press

You can purchase any of these Hellgate Press titles directly by sending us this completed order form.

To order call, 1-800-228-2275
Fax 1-541-476-1479

Hellgate Press

P.O. Box 3727
Central Point, OR 97502

For inquiries and international orders,
call 1-541-479-9464

TITLE	PRICE	QUANTITY	COST
Army Museums: West of the Mississippi	$13.95		
Byron's War	$21.95		
From Hiroshima With Love	$18.95		
Gulf War Debriefing Book	$18.95		
Night Landing	$13.95		
Order of Battle	$17.95		
Pilots, Man Your Planes!	$33.95		
Rebirth of Freedom	$16.95		
The War That Would Not End	$19.95		
Words of War	$13.95		
World Travel Guide	$19.95		
Memories Series			
K-9 Soldiers	$13.95		
Green Hell	$18.95		
Oh, What A Lovely War!	$14.95		
Through My Eyes	$14.95		

SHIPPING INFORMATION

If your purchase is:	your shipping is:
up to $25	$5.00
$25.01–$50.00	$6.00
$50.01–$100	$7.00
$100.01–$175	$9.00
over $175	call

Subtotal	$
Shipping	$
Grand Total	$

Thank You For Your Order!

Shipping Information
Name:
Address:
City, State, Zip:
Daytime Phone: Email:
Ship To: (If Different Than Above)
Name:
Address:
City, State, Zip
Daytime Phone:
Payment Method:
For rush orders, Canadian and overseas orders please call for details at (541) 479-9464
☐ Check   ☐ American Express   ☐ MasterCard   ☐ Visa
Card Number: Expiration Date:
Signature: Exact Name on Card:

For more adventure and military history information visit our Website

Hellgate Press Online

http://www.psi-research.com/hellgate.htm

With information about our latest titles, as well as links to related subject matter.

Hellgate Press Reader Survey

Did you enjoy this Hellgate Press title?
☐ Yes   ☐ No
If no, how would you improve it:
_____
_____
_____

Would you be interested in other titles from Hellgate Press?
☐ Yes   ☐ No

How do you feel about the price?
☐ Too high   ☐ Fair   ☐ Lower than expected

Where did you purchase this book?
☐ Bookstore
☐ Online (Internet)
☐ Catalog
☐ Association/Club
☐ It was a gift
☐ Other: _____

Do you use a personal computer?
☐ Yes   ☐ No

Have you ever purchased anything on the Internet?
☐ Yes   ☐ No

Would you like to see more titles from Hellgate about this subject/period of history?
☐ Yes   ☐ No

Would you like to receive a Hellgate catalog?
☐ Yes   ☐ No
If yes, please fill out the information below:

Name: _____

Address: _____

City, State, Zip: _____

Email Address (optional): _____

After the Storm
A Vietnam Veteran's Reflection

Please send this survey to:
PSI Research
c/o Hellgate Press
P.O. Box 3727
Central Point, OR 97526

or fax it: (541) 476-1479
or email your responses to:
info@psi-research.com

Thank You!